GOD'S PLAN FOR YOUR
FINANCIAL SUCCESS

Also by Charles Ross from Thomas Nelson Publishers

Your Commonsense Guide to Personal Financial Planning

GOD'S PLAN FOR YOUR FINANCIAL SUCCESS

CHARLES ROSS

OLIVER
NELSON

THOMAS NELSON PUBLISHERS
Nashville

Published in Nashville, Tennessee, by Thomas Nelson, Inc.

Scripture quotations noted NKJV are from THE NEW KING JAMES VERSION. Copyright © 1979, 1980, 1982, Thomas Nelson, Inc., Publishers.

Scripture quotations noted NIV are from the HOLY BIBLE: NEW INTERNATIONAL VERSION®. Copyright © 1973, 1978, 1984 by International Bible Society. Used by permission of Zondervan Publishing House. All rights reserved.

Library of Congress Cataloging-in-Publication Data

Ross, Charles, 1957–
    God's plan for your financial success / Charles Ross.
      p. cm.
    Includes bibliographical references.
    ISBN 0-7852-7052-3 (pbk.)
      1. Finance, Personal—Religious aspects—Christianity. I. Title.
HG179.R687   1998
332.024—dc21
          97-51888
          CIP

Printed in the United States of America.

1 2 3 4 5 6 QPK 03 02 01 00 99 98

CONTENTS

FOREWORD

There were three aspects of Martin's dream: one was racism, one was war, and the other was poverty. I think we have made enormous strides on racism and even war, but we haven't really dealt with the poverty question. The challenge is to evolve an economy that includes everybody and accords a fair chance to every American.

Charles Ross, in his book *God's Plan for Your Financial Success*, illustrates a way to achieve independence and success while still maintaining your integrity and following God's plan for your life.

Andrew Young

— 1 —

YOUR ATTITUDE AND MONEY

WHY IS MONEY SO IMPORTANT TO GOD?

One of the greatest challenges that Christians face is reconciling the way they handle money and their faith. As we grow in our knowledge of the Lord, we come to understand that our perspective on and handling of money are character tests. They are indications of where we stand in our relationship with Christ. Our stewardship of money tells a story about what we really believe.

I remember one Sunday at church, I lost my checkbook. I was frantically looking all over for it until one of the pastors found it and handed it to me. After thanking him, I had a new set of worries. Had the pastor looked at my checkbook? Did he see how much I had in it? After several moments I calmed down. I started to think, *Why should I care whether the pastor looked at my checkbook?* Then it dawned on me. *How would I feel if God looked at my bank account? What would he see? Would I be ashamed of how I spent my money?* Well, God is all-knowing. He knows exactly what's in my checkbook. Is he pleased? I tithe, and I give offerings to the church. And I am not ashamed of how I spend the rest of my money.

Do you think God approves of the way you handle your money? What does your checkbook tell about you? I believe people's checkbooks tell a lot more about their spiritual development than their behavior in church does. It is easy for Christians to appear spiritual and "religious" in church: shouting the name of the Lord, clapping loudly, serving on all the "right" ministries and committees. But you can't fake giving! Either you give the money, or you don't.

Why did Jesus spend a good part of his recorded words on this one subject? Why are many of the parables about money? Jesus said, "For where your treasure is, there your heart will be also" (Matt. 6:21 NIV). He knew that we wouldn't give money to anything that we really didn't believe in. He also said, "Whoever finds his life will lose it, and whoever loses his life for my sake will find it" (Matt. 10:39 NIV). To find the true meaning of money, we must give it away; we must lose possession of it.

Jesus linked money and our salvation so closely that two stories in the Bible illustrate the way in which our relationship to money can affect our conversion. Zacchaeus said he would give half his money to the poor and pay back four times over to those he had cheated. What was Jesus' response? "Today salvation has come to this house" (Luke 19:9 NIV).

Earlier in Luke, Jesus encountered the rich young ruler. That young man asked Jesus what he had to do to get eternal life. Most of us would probably have said something like, "Do you believe that Jesus is the Son of God?" And he would have probably said yes. Then you need not *do* anything else. But Jesus didn't say that. He told the young man, "Sell everything you have and give to the poor, and you will have treasure in heaven. Then come, follow me" (Luke 18:22 NIV).

The young man had kept all ten of the commandments. How many of us could claim that? But he couldn't part with what was most important in his life—his possessions, his money. Jesus knew that. So I believe that the rich young ruler lied because he had violated at least two of the Ten Commandments: "You shall have no other gods before Me" (Ex. 20:3 NKJV); and "You shall not covet" (Ex. 20:17 NKJV). That very wealthy man had made his money his security, his god. And since he felt very uncomfortable giving away his possessions, his heart was full of a spirit of covetousness. He was greedy and stingy and lusted after the things that his money had brought him.

You might not be faced with the prospect of giving away all that you have to follow Jesus. God might not require that of you. But if he revealed to you one day that he wanted you to undertake a ministry in a developing country or the city where you live, you might have to leave your job to undertake that ministry. What would you do? Jesus' thoughts on the cost of following him are quite clear. Jesus told his disciples,

> **If anyone would come after me, he must deny himself and take up his cross and follow me. For whoever wants to save his life will lose it, but whoever loses his life for me will find it. What good will it be for a man if he gains the whole world, yet forfeits his soul? Or what can a man give in exchange for his soul? For the Son of Man is going to come in his Father's glory with his angels, and then he will reward each person according to what he has done.** (Matt. 16:24–27 NIV)

Jesus doesn't require all his disciples to get rid of all their possessions, give their money away, and leave their jobs to become traveling missionaries. But he does know each person's god, and the rich young ruler's god was his money and possessions. Jesus might not require it of you, but you must be mentally prepared to leave everything if he deems it necessary to fulfill his will for your life. You must be ready to obey, just as a good soldier must be ready to die for the cause.

Our willingness to give up everything, though, comes with a promise. "I tell you the truth," Jesus said to them, "no one who has left home or wife or brothers or parents or children for the sake of the kingdom of God will fail to receive *many times as much in this age* and, *in the age to come, eternal life*" (Luke 18:29–30 NIV, emphasis added).

Money is important to God because there is a powerful relationship between our true spiritual condition and our attitude and actions concerning money and possessions. How can we be counted on to be good stewards over spiritual rewards, things we can't feel and touch, if we can't be good stewards over things we *can* feel and touch?

The Wrong Attitude Toward Money Is Called Covetousness

If money is so important to God, then what should our attitude be toward it?

The Bible calls the wrong attitude toward money and possessions covetousness, which is a strong, dominant sin in our nature. *Covetousness* is basically to desire, envy, want, or lust after what is not ours. The dictate not to covet is one of the Ten Commandments: "You shall not covet your neighbor's house; you shall not covet your neighbor's wife, nor his male servant, nor his female servant, nor his ox, nor his donkey, nor anything that is your neighbor's" (Ex. 20:17 NKJV).

Our society makes obeying this commandment more difficult because it encourages us to covet or be greedy. Advertising messages try to convince us that we need more and more things. That commandment doesn't imply that we should have no desires and delight in nothing. God initially gave us the desires and filled the world with delightful things for us to enjoy. However, we need to find the proper balance because along with giving us the desires and delightful things, God has also denied us certain things. If we seek what God has set off-limits, simply allowing our desires to go unfettered, we will be overwhelmed by covetousness.

"You shall not steal" appears in Exodus 20:15 (NKJV). Placing a commandment about coveting after one on stealing doesn't seem to make much sense to us. But perhaps God wanted to make sure that we didn't take what wasn't ours by following it up with a statement that indicates there is an "attitude" that will lead to stealing. More than that, covetousness can cause us to hang on tightly to what we have and not use our material blessings to contribute to the kingdom.

Examine the story about the rich farmer who did very well, had a great crop one year, and didn't know where to put it all. Jesus spoke to a crowd,

"Watch out! Be on your guard against all kinds of greed; a man's life does not consist in the abundance of his possessions." And he told them this parable: "The ground of a certain rich man produced a good crop. He thought to himself, 'What shall I do? I have no place to store my crops.' Then he said, 'This is what I'll do. I will tear down my barns and build bigger ones, and there I will store all my grain and my goods. And I'll say to myself, "You have plenty of good things laid up for many years. Take life easy; eat, drink and be merry."' But God said to him, 'You fool! This very night your life will be demanded from you. Then who will get what you have prepared for yourself?' This is how it will be with anyone who stores up things for himself but is not rich toward God." (Luke 12:15–21 NIV)

Jesus was trying to tell his followers not to get caught up in accumulating things because if they did that, then what would happen to eternal issues? If I live my life just to build a bigger house, buy a larger car, wear fancier clothes, and forget God, I'll end up with nothing. *Covetousness* means worshiping desire, committing my life to fulfilling my wants and desires. And that, says our Lord, is a sin.

The Right Attitude Toward Money Is Called Giving

The right attitude toward money is not lusting after more, but having a liberal, free, willing, and sacrificial heart that gives. Jesus said, "It is more blessed to give than to receive" (Acts 20:35 NKJV). If you capture the true spirit of giving, you learn the ways of God's heart. When you learn to give not only your money, but also yourself, you learn what it really means to be a child of God. Once you enter that realm, you move beyond just giving lip service to the letter of God's laws and living in a spirit of increase. How God can use you to get his work accomplished here on earth!

And here's the bonus. You cannot give without receiving. Jesus declared, "Give, and it will be given to you. A good measure, pressed down, shaken together and running over, will be poured into your lap. For with the measure you use, it will be measured to you" (Luke 6:38 NIV). This is the reciprocal law of giving. That is, when you give something, something will come back to you. And the reverse is true; if you don't give, you lose, for there will be no return.

I have found that over the years as I have matured in my giving to my church, I have become more giving in other areas of my life. I have moved beyond the tithe, and I now give offerings as well. God has helped me to become more giving to my wife, children, mother, brother, sisters, and other relatives. I have been able to bless people by purchasing plane tickets, paying bail money, and buying gifts without too much of a thought about price. I have not missed a meal, and I enjoy a comfortable life. Understand that I am not trying to bribe God into giving me the desires of my heart. But as I have a developed a giving heart, I have been able to touch others.

God's provision for the giver in Scripture makes clear that in many cases God blesses us financially when we generously give:

> *One man gives freely, yet gains even more;*
> *another withholds unduly, but comes to poverty.*
> *A generous man will prosper;*
> *he who refreshes others will himself be refreshed.*
> (Prov. 11:24–25 NIV)

> **Whoever sows sparingly will also reap sparingly, and**
> **whoever sows generously will also reap generously.**
> (2 Cor. 9:6 NIV)

God prospers us not only to give us new things to play with or a more beautiful home, but also to allow us to give still more: "You will be made rich in every way so that you can be generous on every occasion, and through us your generosity will result in thanksgiving to God" (2 Cor. 9:11 NIV). God's extra provision is to be used to raise our *standard of living* and to raise our *standard of giving*.

In a later chapter we will talk more about giving, but suffice it to say that to develop the right attitude, you must give. You must give of yourself, your kindness, your time, and your money. Once you learn this, you will let God use you to accomplish a great work here on earth. But the choice is yours. God will not force you to give.

Money: A Blessing

If money were all bad, then all we would have to do is withdraw from using it, and that would be that. But money is also a blessing from God.

God's blessing can be seen in the care of Abram (later, Abraham): "Abram had become very wealthy in livestock and in silver and gold" (Gen. 13:2 NIV). Isaac, Abraham's son, was blessed in a similar fashion: "Isaac planted crops in that land and the same year reaped a hundredfold, because the LORD blessed him. The man became rich, and his wealth continued to grow until he became very wealthy" (Gen. 26:12–13 NIV).

Properly using money enhances our relationship with God and expresses our love for our neighbors. The wise men brought their wealth to Christ in the manger as a means of worship. Wealthy women helped support the band of disciples (Luke 8:2–3). Barnabas used his land investments to aid the early church: "Joseph, a Levite from Cyprus, whom the apostles called Barnabas . . . sold a field he owned and brought the money and put it at the apostles' feet" (Acts 4:36–37 NIV). And a seller of purple named Lydia used her home to benefit the early church (Acts 16:14–15).

There are several ways that God uses money to enhance our relationship with him. He makes sure that we know who owns everything, that we develop the grace of giving, that we learn how to control and use money, and that we learn to trust him.

Acknowledging God's Ownership

God's absolute rights as owner are made exceptionally clear in the Bible. David confessed,

The earth is the LORD's, and everything in it,
the world, and all who live in it. (Ps. 24:1 NIV)

Yours, O LORD, is the greatness and the power
and the glory and the majesty and the splendor,
for everything in heaven and earth is yours.
(1 Chron. 29:11 NIV)

God's ownership of all things enhances our relationship with him. When we know that the earth is the Lord's, then property itself makes us more aware of God. In other words, we get to know the owner by looking at his property. If you were staying in and caring for someone else's home, you would get to know that person through the contents of the home. Many things would remind you of the one who lives there. So it is with our relationship with God. The grass we walk on is his, the flowers we plant are his, the house we live in is his, and the car we drive is his. Everything helps us to recognize that we are just caretakers of what belongs to God.

Becoming aware of God's ownership frees us from possessiveness and anxiety. If we have done all that we can to care for items entrusted to us, then we know that they are in bigger hands. If the car breaks down or the water heater goes out in the home, and we don't know where we are going to get the money to fix it, we need to trust God that he will provide a way for our needs to be met.

When you acknowledge God as owner, the questions that relate to giving will change. No longer will you ask, How much should I give? Rather, you will start asking, How much of God's money should I keep for myself? The difference between these two questions is enormous.

Giving

We need to be converted *from* serving money in order *to* serve *God*. That is why most of Jesus' teachings on money were evangelistic. He called people away from the mammon god to worship the one true God. Would it not be a measure of a potential follower's faith to be instructed at the moment of decision to be willing to sacrifice everything? "Any of you who does not give up everything he has cannot be my disciple" (Luke 14:33 NIV). For too many people salvation comes by reciting three or four statements and a prayer at the front of the church. They leave the issue of Christian stewardship for a later discussion.

But those of us who are truly saved by the blood of Jesus know that salvation produces radical changes in lifestyle and thought. Denouncing the importance of money in our lives is quite a dramatic shift for most of us.

The grace of giving often propels the life of faith. Giving money is an effective way of showing our love to God because it is so much a part of us and reveals what is important to us. God is more concerned with how we treat people than with vain attempts at rituals. He said,

> *Is not this the kind of fasting I have chosen:*
> *to loose the chains of injustice*
>   *and untie the cords of the yoke,*
> *to set the oppressed free*
>   *and break every yoke?*
> *Is it not to share your food with the hungry*
>   *and to provide the poor wanderer with shelter—*
> *when you see the naked, to clothe him,*
>   *and not to turn away from your own flesh and*
>   *blood?* (Isa. 58:6–7 NIV)

If you do these things,

> *The LORD will guide you always;*
>   *he will satisfy your needs in a sun-scorched land*
>   *and will strengthen your frame.*
> *You will be like a well-watered garden,*
>   *like a spring whose waters never fail.* (Isa. 58:11
> NIV)

When we let go of money, we let go of part of ourselves and part of our security. When we give money, we release a little more of our egocentric selves and a little more of our false security. It is our way to obey Jesus' command to deny ourselves: "If anyone desires to come after Me, let him deny himself, and take up his cross daily, and follow Me" (Luke 9:23 NKJV).

Giving frees us from the tyranny of money as we learn to give not only money, but also the things that money can buy. The early Christian community gave houses and land to provide funds for those in need:

> **All the believers were one in heart and mind. No one claimed that any of his possessions was his own, but they shared everything they had. With great power the apostles continued to testify to the resurrection of the Lord Jesus, and much grace was upon them all. There were no needy persons among them. For from time to time those who owned lands or houses sold them, brought the money from the sales and put it at the apostles' feet, and it was distributed to anyone as he had need. Joseph, a Levite from Cyprus, whom the apostles called Barnabas (which means Son of Encouragement), sold a field he owned and brought the money and put it at the apostles' feet.** (Acts 4:32–37 NIV)

We can give cars or sell investments or other items of value to finance mission work, or we can give to someone in the neighborhood who has a need. Money has also given each of us the time to acquire skills. As a carpenter, doctor, lawyer, accountant, electrician, or whatever, you can give of your time to help the community.

Controlling and Using Money

The control and use of money and the things money can buy play a large part in enhancing our relationship with God. Believers who are rightly taught and disciplined from the Word of God are enabled to hold possessions without corruption and use them for the greater purpose of the kingdom of God.

Jesus had many other teachings on the good use of money. He allowed well-to-do women to support his ministry (Luke 8:1–3). He dined with the rich and privileged (Luke 11:37; 14:1). He commended the good Samaritan, who used money generously and drew closer to the kingdom of God (Luke 10:30–37).

Some Christians think we should sell all our possessions and give them to the poor. There is a place for doing that, but it is vastly inferior to the proper management and wise use of resources. It is much better to have wealth and resources in the hands of Christians who are doing God's will.

Abraham, Job, David, and Solomon managed large holdings for the glory of God and the greater public good. Nicodemus, a man of wealth and position, used both for the good of the Christian fellowship. As I stated earlier, because Barnabas had done well in managing his property holdings, he was able to help the early church when the need was acute (Acts 4:36–37).

Christians should become involved in the business world. That is a high and holy calling. It is a good thing for people with the Spirit of God to make money. Believers should also look for opportunities, if it is their calling, to be in positions of power, wealth, and influence. All of this, of course, is in the context of people who are led by the Spirit of God, people who have been taught and are disciplined. We need instruction on how to possess money without *being possessed by money*. We need to learn how to own things without the things owning us. We need to learn how to live simply while managing wealth and power.

The apostle Paul said that he had learned how to live in abundance and in want: "I know what it is to be in need, and I know what it is to have plenty. I have learned the secret of being content in any and every situation, whether well fed or hungry, whether living in plenty or in want." Paul knew that God's work would still get done: "I can do everything through him who gives me strength" (Phil. 4:12–13 NIV).

As I said earlier and will say many more times in this book, money is a blessing when it is used within the context of the life and power of God. Using money to bless others truly draws us nearer to God. We must stand amazed that God would use our small efforts to do his work upon the earth. Resources are funneled into churches and ministries. Projects that advance the kingdom are financed. People are led to Christ. The call of God is upon each of us to use money within the confines of a properly disciplined spiritual life and to manage money for the good of all people and for the glory of God.

Building Trust

When we learn to trust God for our financial lives, we learn to trust him and only him. When the children of Israel gathered manna in the wilderness, they were instructed to gather only a daily supply. When they saved some for the next day (except the Sabbath), it spoiled. They were learning to live in daily trust upon God.

In no way is this comment meant to fly in the face of having retirement plans and savings accounts. The point here is that money can be used by God to build a more trusting bond with him. I remember when I was starting my company and didn't know where my next dollar was coming from. I continued to give my tithes and offerings to my church. My conviction was that God wanted me to start my business to glorify him. If you have ever started a business, you can understand that you need every penny to keep it going. God not only prospered the business, but during that period, my wife and I had two additional children. Sure, the business had its challenges, but never did I miss a meal. I never was in fear of losing my home. The business has been prosperous enough to allow me the time to write my second book and start another company and pursue my ministry. Talk about trust!

God can take something as ordinary as money, which often competes as a rival god, and use it to lead us forward in the kingdom of Christ.

Advancing the Kingdom

If you haven't figured it out yet, money is to be used to advance the kingdom of God. That is what Jesus commanded us to do: "Go therefore and make disciples of all the nations, baptizing them in the name of the Father and of the Son and of the Holy Spirit" (Matt. 28:19 NKJV). Spreading the gospel requires money. Jesus moved about preaching and teaching with a large entourage. The people needed food, shelter, and clothing, and many wealthy individuals supported Jesus' ministry. Nowadays, it still takes money to finance kingdom work. But the key to unlocking our understanding of money resides in two passages in the Bible, Matthew 6:19–24 and Luke 16:1–13. Jesus' statement in Matthew that we cannot serve God and mammon has to be reconciled with the one in Luke that insists we make friends by using "unrighteous mammon" or money.

In the parable in Luke, a man discovered that his business manager or steward had been misappropriating money and fired him. But before his termination became final, the man conjured up a plot to ensure that he would be able to make ends meet once he was on his own. He set out to call on the individuals who owed his employer money. One by one he wrote off anywhere from 20 to 50 percent of their debts. Of course, the plan caused the debtors to be grateful to the steward and to be obliged to help him out later on when he was out of a job. But here is the clincher: his master found out and, instead of having him imprisoned, commended him for his shrewdness.

Even though Jesus never condoned the man's dishonesty, he pointed out that the steward used money to make friends who would likely help him out when he needed it most. In addition, Jesus noted that the children of the world are more knowledgeable than the children of God about how to use money for their own purposes: "The master commended the dishonest manager because he had acted shrewdly. For the people of this world are more shrewd in dealing with their own kind than are the people of the light" (Luke 16:8 NIV).

Then Jesus wrapped up the story by telling his disciples that we should use wealth or money to gain friends who will care for us when money fails and we have fallen on hard times: "I tell you, use worldly wealth to gain friends for yourselves, so that when it is gone, you will be welcomed into eternal dwellings" (Luke 16:9 NIV). We are called to use money to make friends and to advance the kingdom of God.

Moving the kingdom forward means putting mammon to greater use. In Matthew, Jesus warned us: "Do not store up for yourselves treasures on earth," for he knew such treasures are insecure investments, "where moth and rust destroy, and where thieves break in and steal." Instead we are to store up for ourselves "treasures in heaven." The reason is twofold. Heavenly treasures are much more secure investments "where moth and rust do not destroy, and where thieves do not break in and steal." In addition, investing in God's kingdom determines where our spirits will be: "For where your treasure is, there your heart will be also" (Matt. 6:19–21 NIV).

If you concentrate on storing treasures in heaven by making more disciples, then you are focusing on investing in the lives of people. When God blesses you with money, you are not to put all of it into things here on earth because these things have no eternal value. Yes, you need to have money to take care of yourself and your family, but if you want to be in the will of God, then you need to free up as much as you can to advance the kingdom. Money invested to make more disciples is the best possible investment you can make.

The needs of the kingdom are tremendous. You may have a needy friend or neighbor, or an opportunity may present itself to promote the gospel in a remote region of the world. Opportunities will come your way as you let God lead you.

The reality of the conflict between Luke 16:9 and Matthew 6:24 is that we must learn to use money without serving it. And learning to master money is what this book is all about.

SHOULD CHRISTIANS PROSPER?

Should Christians prosper? Let me take the suspense away and say yes! God wants us to prosper so much that he sent his only Son, Jesus, to prove it. If our Father was willing to give us his very best, then why would he hold anything else back from us? Our Father wants us to prosper so that we may fulfill the Great Commission by making more disciples (Matt. 28:18–20). That takes money.

Early on in the Bible, we can read about God's desire for our prosperity: "But remember the LORD your God, for it is he who gives you the ability to produce wealth, and so confirms his covenant, which he swore to your forefathers, as it is today" (Deut. 8:18 NIV). God declared that he gave us the ability to get wealthy as part of his covenant, and his covenant was with our forefathers, such as Abraham. Now Christ died so that the blessings God had promised Israel might be given to the Gentiles too: "Christ redeemed us from the curse of the law by becoming a curse for us, for it is written: 'Cursed is everyone who is hung on a tree.' He redeemed us in order that the blessing given to Abraham might come to the Gentiles through Christ Jesus, so that by faith we might receive the promise of the Spirit" (Gal. 3:13–14 NIV). Furthermore, the apostle Paul wrote, "If you are Christ's, then you are Abraham's seed, and heirs according to the promise" (Gal. 3:29 NKJV). If we find out what blessings were given to Abraham, then we find out what is in store for us:

> *I will make you into a great nation*
> *and I will bless you;*
> *I will make your name great,*
> *and you will be a blessing.*
> *I will bless those who bless you,*
> *and whoever curses you I will curse;*
> *and all peoples on earth will be blessed through you.*
> (Gen. 12:2–3 NIV)

The Abrahamic covenant included blessings to be extended to Abraham's descendants (v. 7), God's protection of Abraham (v. 3), and abundant blessings to Abraham himself, including wealth, fame, and influence. In addition, he would be a source of blessing for others (v. 2). In fact, the verb in the final phrase of verse 2 is grammatically an imperative. Abraham was instructed to be a blessing. Thus, his call was from the outset a missionary mandate encompassing all people.

Then how much wealth was Abraham blessed with? He became "very wealthy in livestock and in silver and gold" (Gen. 13:2 NIV). He became so wealthy that he and his nephew Lot could not live in the same region: "The land could not support them while they stayed together, for their possessions were so great that they were not able to stay together" (Gen. 13:6 NIV).

God's Word tells us that we are heirs of Abraham. That is, the blessings that God gave Abraham are available to us. Our Father wants us to receive the same blessings that he gave to Abraham, and we can receive these blessings if we will follow his law of prosperity.

I believe that God's law of prosperity can be summed up in one verse: "Do not let this Book of the Law depart from your mouth; meditate on it day and night, so that you may be careful to do everything written in it. Then you will be *prosperous* and *successful*" (Josh. 1:8 NIV, emphasis added). *To prosper* is "to achieve economic or financial success." *To succeed* means "to turn out well, to obtain a desired object or end, in other words, to reach one's goals."

It doesn't always follow that if you are prosperous, you are successful. You could become prosperous by inheriting some money, having a good income, or starting a business that becomes very profitable, but you might be miserable. We have all heard of people with money who abuse drugs, commit suicide, or lead a life of misery and shame.

I read in a magazine that Oprah Winfrey felt empty and had low self-esteem, despite having all her money. At the time she was reportedly worth $250 million and earning $40 million a year. She was prosperous, but in her eyes she was not successful. Janet Jackson, part of one of the most successful show business families, earned a whopping $40 million in 1991 from a record contract, but she said in an interview that "just because you have money it doesn't mean you're happy."

You may have a hard time believing that someone can have money and still not be happy. But you can learn something from these people. Individuals can be successful, in other words, hit goals by losing weight, breaking a world record, writing a book, raising God-fearing children, but not be financially successful. There are people like this all over the world, even living next door to you.

You can have success without prosperity or vice versa, but the Lord says in Joshua 1:8 that if you do three things, you will have both. First, you have to *speak* God's Word: "Do not let this Book of the Law depart from your mouth." The Word should stay on your lips; it should be coming out of your mouth at every opportunity. You have to evangelize, go out and witness, and share the gospel with friends, coworkers, relatives, strangers, whoever you come in contact with. Remember Abraham who was told, "And you shall be a blessing" (Gen.

12:2 NKJV). The primary way that you are going to be a blessing to other people is to bless them with words, God's words.

Next, you have to continue to *study* the Bible. You must have a regular study time, preferably daily: "Meditate on it day and night." How are you going to know what to say to people when you are witnessing to them if you don't know God's Word? And to conform yourself to the likeness of God, you need to know more about him. The only source of that knowledge is his inspired Word.

Finally, you have to *do* something: "So that you may be careful to do everything written in it." You have to do God's Word; you must do something to make a difference. The ultimate result is to lead people to Christ. To assist us in discipleship, each of us has been given a gift from God to minister to the Lord's church: "Each man has his own gift from God; one has this gift, another has that" (1 Cor. 7:7 NIV); and "We have different gifts, according to the grace given us" (Rom. 12:6 NIV).

Read the list of spiritual gifts in 1 Corinthians 12:4–11, and let the Holy Spirit reveal to you your gift. Then do something, for the wise put God's words into action (Matt. 7:24), and "Go therefore and make disciples of all the nations" (Matt. 28:19 NKJV). God will indeed make you "prosperous and successful" (Josh. 1:8 NIV). If the Lord grants you wealth, then you will be at peace. Look at Proverbs 10:22 (NIV): "The blessing of the LORD brings wealth, / and he adds no trouble to it." If God didn't want you to prosper, then he wouldn't have made a provision for it in his Word. He definitely would not have sent his Son, Jesus, to die for the sins of humankind.

Remember that God prospers you so that you can be a blessing to other people and advance the kingdom: "You will be made rich in every way *so that you can be generous on every occasion,* and through us your generosity will result in thanksgiving to God" (2 Cor. 9:11 NIV, emphasis added).

POVERTY: A CURSE OR A BLESSING?

Too many people think a mark of spirituality is to drive a broken-down car, have nothing decent to wear, and live in a one-room shack, just barely getting along. They believe that being poor brings them closer to God. But that is not what God has in store for you. Jesus said, "Seek first his kingdom and his righteousness, and all these things will be given to you as well" (Matt. 6:33 NIV). He didn't say subtracted from you; he said given to you. And what exactly would be given? Material blessings because just before that he listed all the things that you shouldn't worry about, including food and clothing: "So do not worry, saying, 'What shall we eat?' or 'What shall we drink?' or 'What shall we wear?' For the pagans run after all these things, and your heavenly Father knows that you need them" (Matt. 6:31–32 NIV).

If God wants to bless us with material things, why are so many people poor? Because poverty is a spirit. Being poor is not about living in a ghetto or growing up in the most run-down part of town. Being poor does not come as a result of high unemployment or the lack of qualifying skills. These things are just the fruit of poverty, not the root of poverty.

Poverty is a destructive spirit that robs human beings of their dreams, goals, motivations, and desires. Being broke is a temporary financial condition, but being poor is a spiritual condition. Poverty is nearly always connected with unrighteousness (not living in right relationship with God). Let me make this clear: it is just as erroneous to think poverty is a sign of spirituality as to think wealth is. God is in ultimate control of both wealth and poverty:

> *The LORD sends poverty and wealth;*
> *he humbles and he exalts.*
> *He raises the poor from the dust*
> *and lifts the needy from the ash heap;*
> *he seats them with princes*
> *and has them inherit a throne of honor.*
> *For the foundations of the earth are the LORD's;*
> *upon them he has set the world.* (1 Sam. 2:7–8 NIV)

The scriptural ideal is specifically stated to be having neither wealth nor poverty but something in between:

Keep falsehood and lies far from me;
give me neither poverty nor riches,
but give me only my daily bread.
Otherwise, I may have too much and disown you
and say, "Who is the LORD?"
Or I may become poor and steal,
and so dishonor the name of my God. (Prov. 30:8–9 NIV)

Historically the unrighteousness of an individual or the nation as a whole brought oppression upon the people of Israel. In 1 and 2 Kings, we see how poverty was a result of God's judgment on the rule of Ahab. He had allowed the entrance of idol worship into the land. That spiritual problem brought physical poverty.

For many years now our government and its political leaders have promoted social programs including welfare, work programs, and job training. Why haven't these programs ended poverty in a nation that unarguably is the most affluent in the world? Why do some remain in poverty, but others do not? There is a spirit involved. If Christians can expose poverty as a spirit, then we can introduce the answer—the power of the gospel.

You can easily recognize the signs of poverty when you know what to look for. Remember it is not just a lack of money. Some individuals who earn $100,000 a year and others who earn $1 million or more still have a spirit of poverty. Here are some major signs of poverty:

Refusing to be taught the Word of God. Consider this advice from the book of Proverbs:

The fear of the LORD is the beginning of knowledge,
but fools despise wisdom and discipline. (Prov. 1:7 NIV)

He who ignores discipline comes to poverty and shame,
but whoever heeds correction is honored. (Prov. 13:18 NIV)

God has given certain instructions in his Word to get people out of poverty. You will have trouble getting your life together until you read the instruction manual—the Bible. Unless you act in faith on the Word of God, God cannot rightly hold back those who would come to steal your abundance. The curses outlined in Deuteronomy come because you have not listened to and acted on the Word of God:

> **All these curses will come upon you. They will pursue you and overtake you until you are destroyed, because you did not obey the LORD your God and observe the commands and decrees he gave you. They will be a sign and a wonder to you and your descendants forever. Because you did not serve the LORD your God joyfully and gladly in the time of prosperity, therefore in hunger and thirst, in nakedness and dire poverty, you will serve the enemies the LORD sends against you. He will put an iron yoke on your neck until he has destroyed you.** (Deut. 28:45–48 NIV)

Following pipe dreams and not working. The book of Proverbs offers these straightforward comments:

> *Lazy hands make a man poor,*
> *but diligent hands bring wealth.* (Prov. 10:4 NIV)

> *The sluggard's craving will be the death of him,*
> *because his hands refuse to work.* (Prov. 21:25 NIV)

> *He who works his land will have abundant food,*
> *but he who chases fantasies lacks judgment.* (Prov. 12:11 NIV)

> *He who works his land will have abundant food,*
> *but the one who chases fantasies will have his fill of poverty.* (Prov. 28:19 NIV)

If you work, you will have your needs met. But if you don't work and have all these ideas on how "you gonna make it," then you will not have God's best. We all know people like that. They have all these ideas about how they are going to strike it rich.

Now don't get me wrong. We should encourage people to pursue their dreams as long as they are God's will for their lives. But when people just talk and do nothing to make dreams become reality, they are just wishfully thinking. The best way to deal with such people is to ask to see their plan. And when you see it, does it make sense?

Not giving to the kingdom of God. Here is more from the book of Proverbs:

> *One man gives freely, yet gains even more;*
> *another withholds unduly, but comes to poverty.*
> *A generous man will prosper;*
> *he who refreshes others will himself be refreshed.*
> (Prov. 11:24–25 NIV)

Giving frees the individual to receive: "Give, and it will be given to you: good measure, pressed down, shaken together, and running over will be put into your bosom. For with the same measure that you use, it will be measured back to you" (Luke 6:38 NKJV).

People with a spirit of poverty are looking for an excuse to hold on to possessions even more tightly. These excuses arise out of the fear that if they give what they have, they won't have anything left. This is not faith in God. It is a "see and then I will believe" mentality. God does not reward doubt. He rewards faith: "Without faith it is impossible to please God, because anyone who comes to him must believe that he exists and that he rewards those who earnestly seek him" (Heb. 11:6 NIV).

When you fail to give, you prevent other people from being blessed by your giving. Since God's way of blessing people is through other people, you block the blessing, and God can't use you. Giving is a true sign that you believe Jesus has risen. Giving demonstrates that you have faith, and when you act on that faith, you start to see results. Faith breaks the spirit of fear that tries to convince you to hold on to your money. Then the spirit of poverty is broken.

Having a get-rich-quick mentality. These passages from the book of Proverbs speak to this issue:

A faithful man will be richly blessed,
but one eager to get rich will not go unpunished.
(Prov. 28:20 NIV)

Do not wear yourself out to get rich;
have the wisdom to show restraint. (Prov. 23:4
NIV)

God is not opposed to your being rich. If he was, he wouldn't have made a provision for it: "But remember the LORD your God, for it is he who gives you the ability to produce wealth, and so confirms his covenant, which he swore to your forefathers, as it is today" (Deut. 8:18 NIV) The admonition of these verses is to avoid making the acquisition of wealth the chief aim of your life by concentrating all energies upon its pursuit: "People who want to get rich fall into temptation and a trap and into many foolish and harmful desires that plunge men into ruin and destruction. For the love of money is a root of all kinds of evil. Some people, eager for money, have wandered from the faith and pierced themselves with many griefs" (1 Tim. 6:9–10 NIV).

Nothing in 1 Timothy 6:9–10 indicates that great possessions are sinful. Yet the apostle made abundantly plain the dangers involved in great possessions: (1) riches make temptation and entanglement more likely; (2) foolish and hurtful desires are encouraged; (3) these desires often lead to destruction; (4) the love of money is a root of all kinds of evil; (5) frequently one falls away from the faith because of the pursuit or protection of riches; (6) wealth is regularly the cause of people's piercing themselves through with many sorrows. People who have been blessed by God with material wealth should never despise the blessing but should heed the warnings.

Now that we know there is a spirit of poverty, how can we beat it? The spirit of poverty is a destructive force; it is a curse that will destroy us. Well, Jesus already delivered us from the curse of poverty. The curse of the Law, which is the penalty for breaking God's Law, includes spiritual death (separation from God), sickness, disease, and poverty. Most people understand that in Christ, they have been redeemed from spiritual death, sickness, and disease. But they don't realize that they have been redeemed from poverty: "Christ redeemed us from the curse of the law by becoming a curse for us, for it is written: 'Cursed is everyone who is hung on a tree'" (Gal. 3:13 NIV).

What exactly is the curse of the Law? The Law refers to the first five books of the Bible called the Pentateuch. And the first curse that God mentioned was recorded in Genesis: "But of the tree of the knowledge of good and evil you shall not eat, for in the day that you eat of it you shall surely die" (Gen. 2:17 NKJV).

Adam did not die physically that day when he and Eve ate of the tree of knowledge of good and evil. It was more than nine hundred years before Adam died, but he did die spiritually. He was separated from God. Adam became spiritually dead by breaking the relationship and fellowship with God through his sin. So spiritual death is a curse of the Law.

In Deuteronomy 28, there are sixty-eight verses: the first fourteen deal with the blessings for obeying God, and the last fifty-four deal with the curses. We discover that sickness and disease are curses of the Law: "The LORD will also bring on you every kind of sickness and disaster not recorded in this Book of the Law, until you are destroyed" (v. 61 NIV). It is also revealed that poverty is a curse of the Law: "The LORD will send on you curses, confusion and rebuke in everything you put your hand to, until you are destroyed and come to sudden ruin because of the evil you have done in forsaking him" (v. 20 NIV). Now that's poverty! So, if poverty is a curse of the Law and Jesus has redeemed us from the curse of the Law, it follows that we have been redeemed from the curse of poverty.

Notice also there are blessings for us today that can be summed up in verse 12: "The LORD will open the heavens, the storehouse of his bounty, to send rain on your land in season and to bless all the work of your hands. You will lend to many nations but will borrow from none."

That was written to Israel under the old covenant. But hear what the new covenant has to say about fulfilling or obeying God's laws and commandments: "Let no debt remain outstanding, except the continuing debt to love one another, for he who loves his fellowman has fulfilled the law" (Rom. 13:8 NIV); and "The entire law is summed up in a single command: 'Love your neighbor as yourself'" (Gal. 5:14 NIV).

Under the new covenant we have a commandment to keep in order to prosper. It's the commandment of love. So if we are walking in love, we have fulfilled God's law. Don't let anyone tell you that it is more spiritual to be poor. God hasn't given us a spirit of poverty. He has redeemed us from the curse of poverty. He has given us his Son, Jesus, who died that we may have life and "have it more abundantly" (John 10:10 NKJV).

WAS JESUS POOR?

There seems to be a pervasive image that Jesus Christ was poor. Many point to this verse as evidence of that: "For you know the grace of our Lord Jesus Christ, that though he was rich, yet for your sakes he became poor, so that you through his poverty might become rich" (2 Cor. 8:9 NIV).

I believe that Jesus became poor but not during his earthly ministry. He became materially poor when he made the supreme sacrifice on the cross at Calvary. Jesus gave up everything at that time—even his clothing. In spite of many pictures to the contrary, Jesus was completely naked when he died on the cross. He couldn't have been more poor than he was at that time. While he hung on the cross, soldiers gambled for the rights to his clothing. But to truly understand Jesus' economic status, let's review first his family's economic situation and then his financial position during his three-year earthly ministry.

Until he was about thirty, Jesus worked in Nazareth as the son of a carpenter. He was also a carpenter (Mark 6:3); Jesus worked for most of his life at that trade. Jesus' family belonged to the middle structure of his society, to the small traders and artisans. A carpenter's son might not have been rich, but he would have had much to be thankful for compared with the majority of the population. In the environment of Nazareth, Jesus would have had many advantages. He was a firstborn male in a Jewish family with a reputable home and business. He would have been guaranteed an education, an inheritance, and many other privileges that most of his contemporaries did not have. He seemed to have been strong, wise, and well respected: "And the Child grew and became strong in spirit, filled with wisdom; and the grace of God was upon Him" (Luke 2:40 NKJV).

Luke's statement that the young Jesus "increased in wisdom and stature, and in favor with God and men" (Luke 2:52 NKJV) is consistent with our image of Jesus' authority. A hometown carpenter does not quite conform to our image of the ideal messianic prince. Nevertheless, in his economic and social conditions, he had much in his growing-up years that others in his day and age would envy.

If we believe that Jesus' birth was an incarnation—the birth of the divine Son of God into the world—then his social and economic identity was not an accident, as perhaps it is for ordinary humans. Unlike you and me, Jesus deliberately chose his economic identity. God's choice expressed something of his character. Our loving heavenly Father took care that his Son had an environment where he could develop, become strong, and be filled with wisdom.

During his earthly ministry, people claim that Jesus was poor because he didn't really have a home: "Foxes have holes and birds of the air have nests, but the Son of Man has no place to lay his head" (Luke 9:58 NIV). Jesus had friends at whose homes he could stay. He really didn't need a home because as the first traveling evangelist, he was constantly on the move. Traveling with his twelve disciples and seventy other men, Jesus was able to meet the needs of the traveling Bible college. And he had a treasurer to keep track of finances: "Judas had charge of the money" (John 13:29 NIV). We all know that Judas would later betray Jesus. His treasurer was also a thief: "He did not say this because he cared about the poor but because he was a thief; as keeper of the money bag, he used to help himself to what was put into it" (John 12:6 NIV).

We have to believe that Jesus knew that Judas was a thief, yet he never fired him. So not only did Jesus need to have the finances to operate daily, but he had to have a surplus to make up for Judas's stealing. I believe that Jesus tolerated the thievery to demonstrate that there was more than enough, for he could handle any financial situation.

The Bible never states that Jesus wanted for anything—food or basic necessities. He stayed at the homes of wealthy individuals whom he often was trying to teach and recruit. Jesus was a complete master of God's law of prosperity. He repeatedly used the law to meet his needs. What poor man could feed four thousand people? Jesus asked, "When I broke the seven loaves for the four thousand, how many basketfuls of pieces did you pick up?" The disciples answered, "Seven" (Mark 8:20 NIV).

Here are some other examples of Jesus' mastery of God's law of prosperity. When Peter and the other disciples had fished all night but came up empty, Jesus was able to produce so many fish that the nets broke: "When he had finished speaking, he said to Simon, 'Put out into deep water, and let down the nets for a catch.' Simon answered, 'Master, we've worked hard all night and haven't caught anything. But because you say so, I will let down the nets.' When they had done so, they caught such a large number of fish that their nets began to break" (Luke 5:4–6 NIV).

When Jesus needed a donkey to ride into Jerusalem on the first Palm Sunday, he didn't have to rent or buy a donkey: "As they approached Jerusalem and came to Bethphage on the Mount of Olives, Jesus sent two disciples, saying to them, 'Go to the village ahead of you, and at once you will find a donkey tied there, with her colt by her. Untie them and bring them to me. If anyone says anything to you, tell him that the Lord needs them, and he will send them right away'" (Matt. 21:1–3 NIV).

The Bible records that at his crucifixion, soldiers drew lots to decide who would win his valuable one-piece robe:

When the soldiers crucified Jesus, they took his clothes, dividing them into four shares, one for each of them, with the undergarment remaining. This garment was seamless, woven in one piece from top to bottom. "Let's not tear it," they said to one another. "Let's decide by lot who will get it." This happened that the scripture might be fulfilled which said,

*"They divided my garments among them
and cast lots for my clothing."*

So this is what the soldiers did. (John 19:23–24 NIV)

If he was poor during his earthly ministry, where did he get a robe that was so valuable that soldiers gambled for it?

Jesus was not poor. He had the purest faith that has ever been seen on this earth. He had absolutely no need for worldly, material assets because he knew that he could apply that faith to God's law of prosperity to obtain whatever he needed.

Jesus knew where his power came from: "I tell you the truth, the Son can do nothing by himself; he can do only what he sees his Father doing, because whatever the Father does the Son also does" (John 5:19 NIV).

But Jesus also said that if the Holy Spirit dwells within us, we can have this same power: "I tell you the truth, anyone who has faith in me will do what I have been doing. He will do even greater things than these, because I am going to the Father. And I will do whatever you ask in my name, so that the Son may bring glory to the Father. You may ask me for anything in my name, and I will do it" (John 14:12–14 NIV).

This power is available to all of us. However, this power that will allow you to live a prosperous life isn't just automatic because you are a Christian. You have to follow God's plan for a successful financial life. Read on to discover more about your personal financial plan.

— 2 —

SETTING FINANCIAL GOALS THAT PLEASE GOD

A life without goals is usually characterized by mediocrity. Things are exciting only for the moment. You find yourself caught up in what feels good now. Any serious financial plan must include realistic goals. To save money and invest, you must be motivated, and goals give you focus and direction. Goals are objectives; they are dreams put into action:

> *To man belong the plans of the heart,*
> *but from the LORD comes the reply of the tongue.*
> (Prov. 16:1 NIV)

> *Commit to the LORD whatever you do,*
> *and your plans will succeed.* (Prov. 16:3 NIV)

The hardest task for most people is prioritizing their goals, that is, determining which ones are the most important. A challenging discipline of the Christian life is that of assigning priorities. Busyness is not godliness, but godliness exhibits itself in a Spirit-controlled life. God wants the best for his children, and the best comes only through obedience: "If you are willing and obedient, / you will eat the best from the land" (Isa. 1:19 NIV).

First in priority must be *your relationship with God:* "Seek his kingdom, and these things will be given to you as well" (Luke 12:31 NIV).

Next, *allegiance to God* is shown in the home, in loyalty to and love for your spouse: "Submit to one another out of reverence for Christ. Wives, submit to your husbands as to the Lord. . . . Husbands, love your wives, just as Christ loved the church and gave himself up for her" (Eph. 5:21–22, 25 NIV). And it is shown in assuming responsibility for the family: "If anyone does not provide for his relatives, and especially for his immediate family, he has denied the faith and is worse than an unbeliever" (1 Tim. 5:8 NIV). This verse is especially important for those who are unmarried and without children because it means looking out for mother, father, sister, and brother.

Then outside the family, there are the privilege and responsibility of serving God through the various ministries of the church as you seek to participate in the *evangelization of the world:* "Therefore go and make disciples of all nations, baptizing them in the name of the Father and of the Son and of the Holy Spirit, and teaching them to obey everything I have commanded you. And surely I am with you always, to the very end of the age" (Matt. 28:19–20 NIV).

The goal that focuses on spouse and family has the most financial components. According to 1 Timothy 5:8, Christians must labor to provide for family members. To fail in this obligation is to deny the faith and to be worse than people with no faith at all. To the sin of slothfulness is added hypocrisy because they claim to be followers of Christ. Biblical faith places a high priority on the family, and meeting the financial needs for the family is part of Christian stewardship.

As Christians, we should manage our personal resources in a responsible way to care for family needs. To fail to fulfill family responsibilities is sin, marking one as untrue to the commitment of faith in Christ. Even nonbelievers provide the necessities of life for their families. And what are the necessities or basic financial goals for every believer? You should provide a place for your family to live, something to eat, and clothes to wear. Additional financial goals include adequate insurance coverage, a plan for retirement, and a regular savings and investment program.

To protect your property and your family, you need the proper amount of life, disability, health, property, and liability insurance (see Chapter 7). Determine how much you need, and buy all you need.

You need to develop a retirement program. Find out from your employer and the government the benefits you will be entitled to when you retire. In addition, look into programs such as individual retirement accounts (IRAs) and 401(k)s to discover other ways you can set aside money for retirement.

A regular savings program is vital. There are many ways to become financially secure, but ignoring a savings program isn't one of them. A good rule of thumb is to save at least 10 percent of your monthly net income. (In a later chapter I will show you how much God's people should save to be able to handle emergencies.) Whatever amount you decide to save, do it on a regular basis.

Some people try to keep their goals in their heads: "Was it $60 or $70 I planned to spend on clothes this month?" The only way to keep up with your goals is to write them down.

The Ford Foundation recently completed a study on achievement. The study reported that 10 percent of the population had specific well-defined goals; 7 percent reached their goals 50 percent of the time; 3 percent reached their goals 90 percent of the time. What made the difference with the latter group? They wrote their goals down.

A goal becomes important to you once you see it on paper. It takes on a life of its own. When God had finished giving the Law to Moses, what did Moses do? "Moses then *wrote* down everything the LORD had said" (Ex. 24:4 NIV, emphasis added).

If Moses hadn't written down the Ten Commandments, today we would still be debating what God actually said to him. We would probably change some of the commandments to accommodate our personal desires.

To have any power or impact, financial goals must be measurable. You must establish a time frame for achievement and a dollar amount needed. (See fig. 1*) Setting time frames for achieving your goals allows you to focus your attention on the one that is most important. In addition, it will give you a sense of urgency that will drive you to accomplish your goals. By attaching a dollar value to a goal, you will know when you have achieved the objective. If you have a financial goal with no time frame or dollar amount, then it is just wishful thinking.

Long-term goals are those that you want to reach five years or more in the future. *Medium-term goals* are those that you desire to achieve within one to four years. *Short-term goals* are those that you seek to accomplish within the next year.

Most people set long-term goals first and then short-term and medium-term goals. For example, suppose you want to retire from your current job in fifteen years with $100,000 in cash savings. A short-term goal may be to save at least $5,000 by the end of the first year. A medium-term goal may be to save $28,000 in four years.

How can you be sure you are setting the proper goals? They should be aligned with your insurance, retirement, and savings-investment programs. But here are some other questions that you might want to ask yourself as you set each financial goal for your life:

- How will achieving this goal advance the kingdom of God?
- Can I honestly ask God's help in striving to reach this goal?
- Will I be a better person for setting and accomplishing this goal?
- Will it help someone else reach his or her goal?
- Will it get me where I want to go?
- Will it violate my conscience?
- Will it violate the rights of others?
- Will my family be able to enjoy the rewards of my accomplishment?
- Am I willing to pay the price to reach this goal?

*Figures are found in the "Work Sheets" section, which begins on page 197.

IMPLEMENTING THE PLAN

Success in reaching your goals means activating your plan. No goal-setting process is complete unless the goals are put into action. Often, the path to financial freedom is littered with would-be millionaires whose only drawback was the inability to implement a plan.

Get a clear fix on what you want to accomplish. Visualize yourself achieving your goal. Imagine your lifestyle, your house, your income and financial security. What do you want your money to do for you? Remember to set a realistic time frame for reaching each goal.

A plan is as essential to success as air is to life. Without a plan, you just wander through life. Get a clear idea of what you want to do, then do it now! Not tomorrow, next week, or next year. Do it now! With a realistic plan and self-discipline, you can attain your dream.

— 3 —

BUDGETING YOUR MONEY

HOW MUCH ARE YOU WORTH?

A financial checkup is part of any financial plan. To know where you're heading, you must know where you are now. Jesus said, "Suppose one of you wants to build a tower. Will he not first sit down and estimate the cost to see if he has enough money to complete it?" (Luke 14:28 NIV).

The reports that will help you determine the "cost" are a balance sheet and a budget. Gathering the information for these reports is the first task. You will need documents such as insurance and investment records and a list of your bank accounts and personal property. Copies of tax returns and employment information will also prove useful. The balance sheet (fig. 2) tells you at any given time what you own, what you owe, and what you are worth. A budget (fig. 3) is a road map that helps you advance toward your goals. A budget doesn't tell you how to *spend* your money. You tell your budget how you *spent* your money.

Most people think that income is a good barometer of financial management. Nothing could be farther from the truth. There are as many people who manage money well on $20,000 a year as there are people who earn $200,000 a year. But the true test of how well you have been able to manage the assets God has entrusted to you is your balance sheet. The item called net worth on the balance sheet represents what you would have to live on if you were to sell all your assets and pay off all your loans. It is an indication of what assets you have managed to accumulate since you started working. It is the most accurate representation of your financial stewardship.

If you have been working fifteen or twenty years, you may discover that you have earned more than $500,000 in income. How much of that have you been able to keep? If seeing that small number in the net worth column doesn't motivate you to start budgeting and saving and investing your money, nothing will!

Becoming financially secure involves sacrifice: spending less than you earn and investing the rest. To get on a wealth-building plan, start keeping records so that you know how much money comes in and how much goes out. You can take shortcuts to financial security, but ignoring a budget program is not one of them. You work hard for your money. Why not spend time managing it? Many of us spend more time washing our cars than we do managing our money.

WHY BUDGET?

You may assume that you have to earn a lot of money to budget. But if you wait until you have enough money to budget, you probably never will. Since most people tend to spend as much as they earn, budgeting takes on more significance. You have to control erratic spending habits.

Look at your household like a business. A business could not survive if the owner didn't plan how to spend its income. You have income and expenses just like a business does. As long as your income exceeds your expenses, you remain in good financial shape.

The major benefit derived from developing and following a budget is the peace of mind that comes when you know that you have a firm grasp on your financial situation and you know where you spend your hard-earned dollars. Having control over your finances will give you confidence in your future.

SETTING UP A BUDGET

Before you embark on a budgeting program, determine your goals, whether they include increasing savings, reducing debt, or getting more bang for your buck out of your insurance programs. (See Chapter 2.)

Next, find out your monthly net income or take-home pay (fig. 3). This is the amount of money you actually receive from your employer after your tithes and all taxes and deductions are taken out and after you've paid your tithes.

We will have a more in-depth discussion on tithing and stewardship in a later chapter, but suffice it to say that Malachi 3:10 makes it very clear that we are to honor God by giving tithes and offerings to support kingdom work. All that we have we owe to God. We are not owners, just stewards or managers of what God has entrusted to us. We should act accordingly.

Adding up your total monthly expenses is the next step. Gather up your receipts, look through your canceled checks, and try to see exactly where your money went last month. Write these figures down and separate them into categories: housing, food, automobiles, and so on. In the next sections, you will find the typical budget percentages for each category on the budget work sheet (fig. 3).

Taxes

If you have ever thought about not paying your taxes or, better still, fudging a little, consider what the apostle Paul had to say about respecting our government: "This is also why you pay taxes, for the authorities are God's servants, who give their full time to governing. Give everyone what you owe him: If you owe taxes, pay taxes; if revenue, then revenue; if respect, then respect; if honor, then honor" (Rom. 13:6–7 NIV).

Paul was sharing the insight Jesus had given his disciples when the Pharisees tried to trap Jesus into declaring nonallegiance to Caesar. That would have been considered blasphemy and could have gotten him charged with a civil crime.

"Tell us then, what is your opinion? Is it right to pay taxes to Caesar or not?" But Jesus, knowing their evil

intent, said, "You hypocrites, why are you trying to trap me? Show me the coin used for paying the tax." They brought him a denarius, and he asked them, "Whose portrait is this? And whose inscription?" "Caesar's," they replied. Then he said to them, "Give to Caesar what is Caesar's, and to God what is God's." (Matt. 22:17–21 NIV)

The message is that we should respect the authority of government. We should pay our taxes; in return we expect a system that works for the well-being of the whole society.

When looking at this item in your budget, make sure you are not overpaying taxes. Many people report that the only way they can save money is to overpay their taxes and get a refund. That is not good stewardship. You may need that extra money throughout the year to take care of other family expenses. You're loaning it to the government but receiving no interest on it.

If you don't know how many exemptions you need to claim to have the correct amount taken from your paycheck, here is what you can do. Look at last year's tax return, and make sure you pay at least 100 percent of the total amount of taxes that you owed for that year. Divide that amount by the number of pay periods in the year, then instruct your employer to deduct that amount from your paycheck. For example, if your total federal tax bill came to $5,000 and you get paid twice a month, you would have your employer deduct $208.33 every pay period ($5,000 divided by twenty-four).

Housing (30 percent)

I realize that 30 percent is a very low number, given the fact that it includes other items, but I will always be conservative about expenses. I understand that too many people stretch themselves to buy a house. Your home should not cost more than 38 percent of your net income. This amount includes your mortgage payment, taxes, insurance, and utilities. If your budget goes over in one category, you have to compensate in another. You may be able to spend 40 percent of your net income on housing, but perhaps you don't have a car note or you have little credit card debt. It all has to balance out.

Consider these other spending tips. Try to get on the budget plan for electricity and gas. You want to try to fix your expense items in your budget so that you can predict the payment. Take all the proper discounts for home owner's or renter's insurance. (See Chapter 7.) Don't forget that you will have to maintain your home, so factor that cost into the budget. This amount may average 5 to 10 percent of your total monthly mortgage payments.

Food (12 percent)

Overspending on food is easy to do. With the increasing pressure on supermarket chains to be profitable, they have devised layouts to increase the time you spend in the store because they know that the more time you spend in the store, the more you will spend. Reducing or just controlling your spending in this category will require planning. Of course, one of the best ways to limit spending is to plan your meals in advance. If you do this, you will shop only for items to complete the menus, and you will make better use of your time and money. These other tips may be useful:

- Always shop with a written list.
- Never go shopping when you are hungry.
- Take a calculator along, and add up items as you shop to stay on budget.
- Shop at one of the warehouse stores (such as Sam's).
- Check out advertised specials.
- Use coupons, but use them only for items you would normally buy.
- When possible, purchase groceries in bulk quantities (cups, napkins, paper plates, etc.).
- Do not take your children with you. Studies show that parents tend to spend more money when children tag along.

- Make sure that the cashier rings up the items correctly.
- Compare prices of store brands to prices of national name brands.

Automobiles (15 percent)

A lot of folks find a car that they like and then try to squeeze it into their budget. That is not the most cost-efficient way to buy a car. The first consideration should be to determine the car payment that will fit into your budget, then find a car to match the payment. And some people get into trouble with car payments because of something called leasing. Many people have entered into lease agreements because the monthly payments are less than if they financed the car to buy it. Leasing allows people to purchase a more expensive car than the budget will allow because monthly payments are based on the residual value of the car (the car's value at the end of the lease), which is going to be less than if they were financing it to own it.

To get the maximum value out of your car, plan on owning it at least ten years. You want to have car payments for the least amount of time, no more than four years. Why? Because to achieve many of your financial goals, you are going to need periods of time in your life when you don't have a car payment. Just think what you could do with $400 a month that is not going toward a car. If you simply save the money without earning any interest, you'll have $4,800 in a year and $24,000 in five years. If you invest $400 each month in a conservative growth mutual fund yielding just 12 percent, it could grow to almost $33,000 in five years.

When buying a new car, always negotiate from the dealer's cost up, not from the manufacturer's suggested retail price, or MSRP. You can find out the dealer's cost by using *Consumer Report*'s New Car Pricing Service (800-933-7700). Many credit card companies and credit unions offer similar services. These services, for a nominal fee, will provide you with the dealer's cost and the MSRP for the base price of any new car as well as how much the dealer pays for the options and their retail cost. Here are some additional new car buying tips:

- Always bargain, starting with the dealer invoice.
- Don't talk price about your trade-in until you have a firm price for your new car.
- Don't accept "good for today" prices. A legitimate quote is good tomorrow or the next day as well.
- Never answer questions like, "How much do you want to pay?"
- Don't buy an extended warranty.

Maintenance

Unless you are able to work on your car, I believe that the best way to save on car maintenance costs is to find an honest and reputable mechanic to do the work. If you can't do all the repairs, perhaps you can perform the routine maintenance items, such as oil change, lubrication, and tune-ups. Most cars now come with a list of routine maintenance activities. You should follow the manufacturer's suggestions for maintenance. Regular maintenance will extend the life of your car and alert you to any problems before they become severe. When large repairs need to be done, you should try to get at least three quotes.

If you recently had work done on your car, you probably wondered whether car repair costs are getting out of hand. Well, they are, but you can fight back if you know how to get a fair price. At the least, you have to know how repair shops set their prices. They take three factors into consideration: (1) the mechanic's hourly rate, which can range from $40 to $70 an hour; (2) the cost of the parts, including a markup; and (3) the time to do the job.

Car repair shops, including dealerships, consult manuals such as *Mitchell's Parts and Labor Estimating Book* to determine how much time a repair should take. So, if it takes two hours to install a fuel pump and the dealer uses a $50-an-hour labor rate, the repair will cost you $100 in labor, not including the cost of the part.

To find out if you are paying a fair price, search your library for a copy of a flat-rate manual such as *Mitchell's*. Then call around to parts stores to find out the retail price for the part you want repaired. Using an average of $50 an hour for labor, find out what the total bill should come to. Then call several car repair shops, and get estimates. After you select a shop to make the repairs, get written estimates that include how long the job will take and how much parts will cost. Ask questions about estimates that are out of line with your research. And if you are not comfortable with the mechanic's diagnosis of your car's problem, get a second opinion. When you take in your car to be repaired, tell the mechanic you want all the old parts.

Insurance (5 percent)

Families seem to overpay or underpay for insurance because they don't have a method for determining whether they have the proper coverage. Most people need several forms of insurance, including life, health, auto, home, and disability. To make sure you are on target with your insurance coverage, see Chapter 7.

Debts (5 percent)

Most families have a problem with this category because they generally are living a more expensive lifestyle than their budget will allow. They finance this lifestyle by using credit cards. The guideline budget can include a 5 percent debt level, but if you are spending 15 percent or more of your net income on debt payments, then you are in over your head. You should stop using credit immediately and start living on cash.

How to Tell If You're in Credit Trouble

The first steps toward getting out of debt are the most obvious and the most difficult ones to take. Admit that you have a problem, then stop borrowing. Determine how much debt you have. List all the unpaid balances you owe (fig. 4), add them up, and ask yourself, Can I pay them off in one year?

Here are other telltale signs of credit trouble:

- You pay the minimum amounts or less each month on your charge cards.
- You've reached your credit limits.
- You no longer contribute to a savings account, or you

have no savings at all.
- Creditors are sending you past due notices.

If some of these problems sound familiar, you're in trouble. But there is a way out.

What to Do to Get Out of Credit Trouble

First of all, don't panic. Do your best to live on cash, pay off what you owe, and concentrate on changing your spending habits. Instead of defining credit in terms of minimum monthly payments, look at total outstanding balances. If you have to continue to charge on your accounts, pay off all new charges on your accounts and the interest, and try to pay off a portion of the previous month's balance. Next, develop a budget. Most people who avoid excess debt budget their money. A budget is a snapshot of where your money goes when it leaves your hands. To help balance your budget, you may have to cut some expenses. Maybe you're carrying too much insurance. Consider a second or temporary job to generate additional income and help pay off the debt.

Where to Get Help

If your credit problems become so severe that you need professional advice, there are 350 nonprofit consumer credit counseling services nationwide whose advice is available free of charge or for a small fee. Credit counseling centers are often better able than you are to negotiate with creditors for greater concessions on interest rates, fees, and penalties. These centers also conduct seminars teaching the wise use of credit. You can contact the Consumer Credit Counseling Service (CCCS) by looking it up in your local telephone directory or by calling 1-800-388-CCCS for the name and location of the CCCS office near you. Be advised that this service doesn't offer Christian counseling, so compare the advice you receive against God's Word.

Beware of private credit repair centers. Their fees are often high, and the promised credit "fix" may not be possible. If you are considering such a service, make sure you get what spokespersons say they will do for you and how much it will cost in writing.

In addition, check the references of the center with previous clients. Using credit wisely is a key to managing your finances to the glory of God.

Your Credit Report

One of the more interesting parts of your credit history is not what is on your credit report (fig. 5) but what is *not* on it. You may be disappointed or relieved to know that your rent, utility bills, and doctor and lawyer fees are often not reported. But new areas are always being added to the list of reported items. Until recently, American Express did not report negative information to credit bureaus. Now the company reports negative data and positive data when requested.

Interpreting your report can be a challenge. Some bureaus use a system called common language, which ranks bill-paying style on a scale from one to nine. The rating is supplied by the creditor, not the credit agency. Number one is the best rating, indicating you pay your bills on time within thirty days or as agreed. The worst rating is a nine, which indicates bad debt, placed for collection, or bankruptcy.

How to Correct Errors in Your Credit Report

The credit bureau gathers the information in your credit file. What is in your file is the result of reports from lenders. Some information the bureau receives can be wrong. To correct mistakes, inform the bureau in writing. Any time you dispute an item, the credit bureau must investigate. If it cannot verify the facts by going back to the original source, the information must be deleted.

If the information is accurate, but there are certain facts about the situation you want known, you can write your version of the incident. This document then becomes part of your record and must be shown to all lenders who request your file.

If you have questions about your credit report or if you want to receive a copy of it, contact the credit bureaus listed on page 43. Be prepared to give the following information:

Full name (including Jr., Sr., etc.)
Social security number
Current and previous addresses within the last five years
Date of birth
Signature
Home telephone number

Equifax Information Service Center
P.O. Box 740241
Atlanta, GA 30374-0241
800-997-2493

Experian National Consumer Assistance Center
P.O. Box 2104
Allen, TX 75013-2104
888 EXPERIA (888-397-3742)

Trans Union Corporation
Consumer Disclosure Center
P.O. Box 390
Springfield, PA 19064-0390

What the Bible Says About Debt

There is some confusion about what the Bible says about debt. First, let's discuss what the Bible *does not say* about debt. The Bible does not say it is a sin to borrow money: "Give to the one who asks you, and do not turn away from the one who wants to borrow from you" (Matt. 5:42 NIV). I believe that if God wanted to settle the issue, he would have made it one of the Ten Commandments. But God has laid down principles to guide us in the use of debt. The Bible does not say it is wise to borrow: "The rich rules over the poor, / And the borrower is servant to the lender" (Prov. 22:7 NKJV). Always it was considered a curse to be in debt. Being free from debt was considered a blessing. In Deuteronomy 28, there are sixty-eight verses. The first fourteen deal with the blessings for obedience; the other fifty-four focus on the curses for disobedience. The blessings for obedience can be summed up in this verse: "The LORD will open the heavens, the storehouse of his bounty, to send rain on your land in season and to bless all the work of your hands. You will lend to many nations but will borrow from none" (Deut. 28:12 NIV). Notice the last sentence; to be able to lend was considered a blessing. But look at this portion of God's Word dealing with the curses for disobedience: "The alien who lives among you will rise above you higher and higher, but you will sink lower and lower. *He will lend to you, but you will not lend to him.* He will be the head, but you will be the tail" (Deut. 28:43–44 NIV, emphasis added). Borrowing money was never considered a positive: "Let no debt remain outstanding, except the continuing debt to love one another, for he who loves his fellowman has fulfilled the law" (Rom. 13:8 NIV). God doesn't want us to be slaves to anyone or anything. He wants us to be obedient to serving him.

The Bible also does not say it is a sin to loan money; however, loaning money will change your relationship with the borrower. If you have ever lent money to someone, what is the first thing you are thinking about whenever you see him or her? *When are you going to pay me back?* And you get really upset if the borrower tells you that he or she is going shopping, out to eat, to a ball game, or on vacation. Your reaction? *You're using my money!*

I believe that it is better to give money than to lend it. Unless you have a written contract, you may not get your money back. When someone asks to borrow money, I have made it a practice to say that I can't lend $500 but I can give $100. I am not expecting to get the money back; it is a gift. Jesus said, "If you lend to those from whom you expect repayment, what credit is that to you? Even 'sinners' lend to 'sinners,' expecting to be repaid in full. But love your enemies, do good to them, and lend to them without expecting to get anything back. Then your reward will be great, and you will be sons of the Most High, because he is kind to the ungrateful and wicked" (Luke 6:34–35 NIV).

We should give because the would-be borrowers may need for us to witness to them in a time of need. The last thing we might feel like doing if they have borrowed money from us and not repaid it is to share Jesus with them. So to prevent having any animosity toward them, I believe it is better to give than to lend. But what is interesting is that people rarely take me up on my gift. I can't figure out why.

Now, let's consider what the Bible *does say* about debt. It is a curse, not a blessing, to borrow, and all borrowing has to be repaid: "The wicked borrow and do not repay, / but the righteous give generously" (Ps. 37:21 NIV). For followers of Christ, bankruptcy should not be an option. We should work out a repayment schedule with our creditors.

In addition, all borrowing should be paid promptly:

> *Do not withhold good from those who deserve it,*
>   *when it is in your power to act.*
> *Do not say to your neighbor,*
>   *"Come back later; I'll give it tomorrow"—*
> *when you now have it with you.* (Prov 3:27–28 NIV)

Many people routinely pay their bills thirty to sixty days beyond the due date. Businesspeople who deal with churches tell me that many of them are late with their payments for goods and/or services. That is not God's way. What type of witness is it if God's people do not honor obligations and pay them late or don't pay them at all?

Scripture reveals that it is not a good idea to co-sign for someone, that is, to be responsible for a debt should the borrower default:

> *My son, if you have put up security for your neighbor,*
> *if you have struck hands in pledge for another,*
> *if you have been trapped by what you said,*
>   *ensnared by the words of your mouth,*
> *then do this, my son, to free yourself,*
>   *since you have fallen into your neighbor's hands:*
> *Go and humble yourself;*
>   *press your plea with your neighbor!*
> *Allow no sleep to your eyes,*
>   *no slumber to your eyelids.*
> *Free yourself, like a gazelle from the hand of the*
>   *hunter,*
> *like a bird from the snare of the fowler.*
> (Prov. 6:1–5 NIV)

The Federal Trade Commission reports that cosigners end up taking over the payments of about half of all loans that have been co-signed. The Bible further states, "He who is surety for a stranger will suffer, / But one who hates being surety is secure" (Prov. 11:15 NKJV). Cosigners will end up suffering for agreeing to be the collateral for someone's loan: "A man lacking in judgment strikes hands in pledge / and puts up security for his neighbor" (Prov. 17:18 NIV). Cosigners are said to have poor judgment, and to top it all off, they could lose their property and other assets:

> *Do not be a man who strikes hands in pledge*
> *or puts up security for debts;*
> *if you lack the means to pay,*
> *your very bed will be snatched from under you.*
> (Prov. 22:26–27 NIV)

I have heard of mothers, fathers, brothers, sisters, daughters, sons, close relatives, friends, and neighbors who have run out on people naive enough to co-sign a loan for them. Cosigners end up having to make payments on a car, boat, house, or other piece of property. By co-signing, they in essence have put their immediate family in jeopardy. Think about it. If the bank didn't think the people were creditworthy enough to lend them money, why should others?

Finally, borrowing may deny God an opportunity to work in our lives. He may have another way for providing for the item we want. God's love stems from a plan infinitely superior to anything human beings could have devised: "'For my thoughts are not your thoughts, / neither are your ways my ways,' declares the LORD" (Isa. 55:8 NIV).

Entertainment/Recreation (5 percent)

Who says you can't have fun on a budget? We need to learn to have fun. God calls for us to rest and relax. But we are all so busy that we often don't know when we should take it easy. However, we need to do it in a way that doesn't drive us deeper into debt. Many Christians finance their "fun" with debt. If you do that, you will not be having fun for long.

When planning vacations, try to schedule them during the "off-seasons" so that you will not pay higher prices. Ask the agent for the lowest possible airfare and some alternatives. Plan your trips far enough in advance so that you can shop for discounts. Instead of a long vacation, think about a three- or four-day stay, and spend the balance of your vacation at home. Discover low-cost or no-cost ways to relax in your hometown.

Clothing (5 percent)

For children ages six or seven and younger, shop at consignment shops. These stores offer merchandise that they are trying to sell for other people. You will find great deals. When children are young, they tend to grow out of their clothes and rarely wear them out. The stores have items for adults too.

Shop outlet stores. This is a billion-dollar business. Many name brand clothing manufacturers have outlet shops that are generally located on the outskirts of town away from the malls. These stores sell products at 30 to 40 percent off. Also when shopping for clothes, make a list of the items you want to buy, and then buy them during the off-season. Talk to your friends who may have kids slightly older than yours. You might be able to use some of their children's clothes that no longer fit.

Savings (10 percent)

You have heard it before—pay yourself first. If you don't, borrowing will become a way of life. Many people get into credit trouble not because they use their credit cards to support a lavish lifestyle but because they have no savings. When an emergency arises—and believe me, almost every month something unexpected happens—then they have to tap that credit line to take care of it. The water heater goes out, the car goes on the blink, you have to go out of town on short notice, or any one of a number of other things can cause you to have to go into debt. Over a period of time the credit card balance shoots up to $3,000 or more, and you don't know where the money went.

The best way to save is through payroll deduction. Your employer deducts a set amount from your paycheck, and it is deposited in your savings account. If your employer doesn't provide this service, then ask your bank to draft your checking account a day or so after your paycheck is deposited and put it in a savings account. Many people try to write a check to their savings account each month, but the money never seems to make it to the savings account. Think about it. The government gets tax money by deducting a little each month from your paycheck. If the IRS relied on most Americans to send a check on April 15, the government would shut down.

I have heard people say that they can't leave the money alone once they have deposited it in their savings account. They are always dipping into the account. Listen, if you don't have the discipline to deposit money in your savings account and not touch it, then you will never, ever be financially independent. And if this is really a problem for you, then you need to pray to God that the temptation will be taken from you. God can do that! But you need to ask him for help.

Medical Expenses (5 percent)

Place in your budget the amount of your deductible. You know that you will have to pay that before the insurance pays anything. If your deductible is $250 a year, spread that amount over twelve months, or $20 a month. Do not sacrifice your family's health due to lack of planning. Make sure that your family members go to the doctor for regular checkups and that you practice preventive medicine. Don't be afraid to get second opinions. Doctors and hospitals vary in what they charge.

Miscellaneous (8 percent)

This category includes all the items that did not fit in the other categories. You might have to add additional ones that are unique to your situation, such as child support and alimony.

I would like to comment on allowances. Spouses need to feel that they have money that they don't have to be accountable for. Each spouse should get the same weekly allowance, and it should not be based on salaries. Each person needs the freedom to spend a certain amount of money as he or she sees fit. The amount should be ample enough to take care of parking, lunches, tolls, or other regular weekly expenses.

Now, subtract your monthly expenses from your net income. Do you have anything left? Good! If not, you are spending more than you earn. You need to cut expenses or find ways to increase your income if you're going to stay in good financial health.

IMPLEMENTING YOUR BUDGET

Many people cash their paychecks, put a little in the checking account, and pocket the rest. To become a better money manager, try depositing all of your income into your checking account and paying your bills and expenses by check. This method will allow you to keep track of your income and expenses and will also make it easier later when you have to review your budget and make adjustments. If you have a computer, you can save a lot of time by using one of the many money management software packages. Two I recommend are Quicken and Microsoft Money.

Another idea is to use an expense diary. An expense diary, which you can get from any office supply store, helps you track expenses, small and large, on a daily basis. A pocket-sized diary is easy to carry, and you can record expenses and store receipts in it. Maintaining your checkbook will support your expense diary records. Noting your expenses will be important for completing your budget and doing your taxes at tax time. Impulse buying can ruin the best budget plan. By depositing all of your income in a checking account, you keep the money out of your hands so that you can't spend it. If you are already using this system, good for you. If not, why not give it a trial run?

REVIEWING AND EVALUATING YOUR BUDGET

Developing a budget and maintaining it aren't always easy. Budgets, like cars, require regular maintenance. For your budget to run smoothly, you have to take the time to review and evaluate it. Unexpected expenses or sudden spending urges can reduce a perfectly sensible, useful budget to shambles.

Set aside time each month to review your budget, maybe at the same time you balance your checking account. Are you spending too much on entertainment? Maybe you need to save more. Except for your tithing and savings pledges, consider your budget flexible enough to adjust to changing times.

Now that your finances are laid out, you may have to decide what to curtail or give up to reach your goals. Don't make it too painful. But if it doesn't hurt a little, you are probably not trying hard enough. Learn to live within your budget.

COMMON MONEY MANAGEMENT MISTAKES

Avoiding major mistakes in money management is just as essential as making the right moves. People make some common errors. Watch out for the following ones.

Limited Family Involvement

Having only one family member involved in financial matters is courting disaster. Even though one spouse may be responsible for decision making, both spouses should meet with their accountants, bankers, insurance agents, stockbrokers, and lawyers.

No Written Goals

When you consider your financial goals, you need to place a dollar amount and a time frame on each objective. For example, if you plan to buy a house, you need to know how much you will need for a down payment and when you plan to buy. In addition, once you have financial goals on paper, you must weigh their relative importance.

No Budget

Not having a budget is a serious mistake. It is very difficult to become financially secure without knowing how much you earn and spend. To get a better grip on your money, be sure to have a written budget. If you don't have it in writing, you can easily forget whether you planned on spending $100 or $150 on food this month. Budgets work!

No Money for Emergencies

You should have a savings fund equal to six months of expenses. That way, if you become unemployed, get sick, or need extra cash, you will not have to borrow. To get your savings fund started, decide how much you can afford and start saving right now, no matter how small the amount may be.

No Tax Planning

It is wise to have a plan to reduce your taxes. A sound strategy is to do what CPAs call tax planning. Find ways to structure your affairs to minimize the taxes paid. As a matter of fact, now is a good time to consult with your tax preparer concerning this year's taxes.

Every year after you have completed your tax return, consult with your tax preparer to develop ways to reduce your taxes for the next year. It might mean converting your hobby to a business to take advantage of business deductions, or it might involve contributing to the company's profit-sharing plan. Becoming financially secure requires knowledge of the tax laws.

Not Using Employee Benefits

As a wise money manager, you should be aware of all your benefits. Many employees, for instance, don't know whether they have group life insurance or the amount of coverage. Many don't compare coverage that might be duplicated, such as with health insurance. One spouse may have a better health insurance plan than the other, but because they have always used one particular plan, they have never bothered to compare to determine if they can lower their health insurance premiums.

Another area that employees neglect is profit-sharing plans such as 401(k)s. These plans allow you to save for retirement and reduce your taxes. The human resources department at your company or your state's department of insurance may be able to help you decide which plan is right for you.

Not Spreading the Risk

Often people invest too much money in one area. A common practice is to obtain a lot of shares of company stock. That is not a bad strategy, but having all your investment money in one stock can be risky. If you don't have money in a money market account, certificates of deposit, mutual funds, or real estate, now is the time to give your investments a fresh look.

Many investors try to decide where the market is going and then invest in vehicles that would benefit from that scenario. But today, people are having trouble predicting in what direction the economy is going. It pays to spread your money around; it's called diversification.

LIVING WELL ON LESS

With advance planning and the right investment moves, you can take a cut in income, change careers, or stay home with the baby and still make ends meet.

First, get a grip on your budget. And above all, avoid buying on credit. You may have to postpone vacations for a while or take less-expensive ones.

To develop a clear picture of your income and expenses, you must decide which expenses are essential and which ones can be cut. You may be able to make significant budget cuts by postponing home improvements, moving to a less-expensive neighborhood, or refinancing your mortgage.

Supplementing Your Income

Planning several years ahead for this kind of change in lifestyle is ideal. If you don't have the luxury of a long lead time before your income drops, here are some options to consider.

Think about making an early withdrawal from your individual retirement account (IRA) or drawing on your savings. There are times when using these funds is a good idea. A career change is one of these times.

If you're young, you can rebuild your savings later. If you view the drop in income as permanent, consider drawing down your capital by the amount you pay to gain a more fulfilling job or a more satisfying life.

Pursuing Investment Options

Before leaving your job, you would be wise to consider making changes in your investments. For example, you may want to start shifting your investments from low-dividend, high-growth securities to a portfolio that features high income.

If you are not inclined to take risks, invest in short-term certificates of deposit and Treasury securities. Investments with potential for fluctuations in principal are not worth the risk if you need the money in a year or less.

When starting your own business, limit outside investments to a money market account. Beyond that, direct most of your assets to the new business. Your profit potential is far greater when you own a business.

Losing Fringe Benefits

Fringe benefits that accompany your present job can be worth hundreds of dollars each month. Leaving one employer for another may enable you to pick up a comparable benefits package. But becoming self-employed or leaving the workforce altogether may present a problem if you have to pick up the tab for these benefits.

Look at your pension benefits. If you are entitled to a lump sum pension distribution when you leave your job, you can roll it over to an IRA within sixty days. If you don't roll it over, you will pay tax on it as well as a 10 percent penalty if you're under fifty-nine years of age. If you will no longer be covered by a pension plan, you will have to provide one for yourself. An IRA is one alternative.

Replacing Your Health Insurance Coverage

Signing up for benefits under your spouse's plan is the best way to replace your health insurance after leaving your job. If you are forced to buy coverage on the open market, you are in for a shock. Without the benefit of group rates, a family plan could cost as much as $200 to $300 a month.

You can get temporary relief under a new federal law called the Consolidated Omnibus Budget Reconciliation Act of 1985 (COBRA). This act requires most employers to let you continue getting group benefits when you leave your job, provided you pick up the premiums plus a 2 percent administration fee.

It's a good idea to buy disability insurance before you leave your job because you may have trouble qualifying later. Update your life insurance coverage too.

Whatever your reasons for deciding to live on less, the longer the lead time before you make the switch, the better off you will be.

— *4* —

GIVING

THE ORIGIN OF TITHING

We may not know for sure who the first tither was until we get to heaven. The Bible seems to indicate that Abraham was the first. But take note. The first offering was given by Cain, the firstborn child of Adam and Eve: "In the course of time Cain brought some of the fruits of the soil as an offering to the LORD" (Gen. 4:3 NIV).

With Abraham, we are first introduced to the concept of tithing—giving a tenth. It is interesting that Abraham is the first example of tithing, for Abraham was also the apostle Paul's example for justification by faith: "Consider Abraham: 'He believed God, and it was credited to him as righteousness'" (Gal. 3:6 NIV). Prior to the Law, Abraham believed (trusted or had faith in) God, and God "credited it to him as righteousness" (Gen. 15:6 NIV). Because of his faith in God, Abraham was considered righteous before God and therefore acceptable to God, based on God's grace. Abraham was also James's example for what he meant by justification by works—actual obedience: "And the scripture was fulfilled that says, 'Abraham believed God, and it was credited to him as righteousness,' and he was called God's friend. You see that a person is justified by what he does and not by faith alone" (James 2:23–24 NIV).

The first time the word *tithe* appears in the Bible is in Genesis 14: "And he [Abraham] gave him [Melchizedek] a *tithe* of all" (v. 20 NKJV, emphasis added). Thus, tithing was practiced more than five hundred years before the Mosaic Law. Abraham started it, and Moses commanded it: "There bring your burnt offerings and sacrifices, your tithes and special gifts, what you have vowed to give and your freewill offerings, and the firstborn of your herds and flocks" (Deut. 12:6 NIV). And Christ himself upheld it: "Woe to you Pharisees, because you give God a tenth of your mint, rue and all other kinds of garden herbs, but you neglect justice and the love of God. You should have practiced the latter without leaving the former undone" (Luke 11:42 NIV).

How did Abraham come to give Melchizedek 10 percent of what he had? Abraham's nephew Lot, who foolishly had pitched his tent toward Sodom (Gen. 13:12), got caught in the crossfire of a war between the king of Sodom and other kings. Lot ended up losing both his possessions and his freedom. Word got back to Abraham, who decided to rescue his nephew. The success of Abraham, who had only 318 men, in defeating all the kings was incredible. Not only did Abraham subdue the kings and take their possessions, but he rescued Lot in the meantime, recovering all his goods: "He recovered all the goods and brought back his relative Lot and his possessions, together with the women and the other people" (Gen. 14:16 NIV). What happened next was amazing. Then "Melchizedek king of Salem" and "priest of God Most High" brought out bread and wine and blessed Abraham, saying,

> *Blessed be Abram by God Most High,*
> *Creator of heaven and earth.*
> *And blessed be God Most High,*
> *who delivered your enemies into your hand.* (Gen. 14:19–20 NIV)

That was where tithing came into the picture. Then Abraham gave Melchizedek a tenth of everything.

Some Bible commentators think that when Melchizedek blessed Abraham and acknowledged God as the Creator of the universe and Source of all blessings, he put into words what Abraham had felt all along. Further, the writer in Hebrews told us that Melchizedek was made "like the Son of God" (Heb. 7:3 NKJV). What Abraham saw and heard, then, was a figure of the Lord Jesus Christ, "one in the order of Melchizedek" (Heb. 7:11

NIV). Abraham responded to the word of Melchizedek as if it were a word from the Spirit of God.

How did Abraham know to give a tenth? Well, we really don't know. Perhaps Abraham, a man justified by faith, knew in his heart what to do. The apostle Paul spoke of the Gentiles who knew nothing of the Law but nonetheless had "the requirements of the law . . . written on their hearts, their consciences also bearing witness, and their thoughts now accusing, now even defending them" (Rom. 2:15 NIV). In other words, the law of God is already inherent in every person's nature. It is called conscience. All people have a conscience, even those who are not born again: "Since what may be known about God is plain to them, because God has made it plain to them. For since the creation of the world God's invisible qualities—his eternal power and divine nature—have been clearly seen, being understood from what has been made, so that men are without excuse" (Rom. 1:19–20 NIV).

A naive notion that those who have never explicitly heard the gospel are not under condemnation is corrected in this passage. What may be intuitively known about God has been placed in the minds (heart, conscience) of all people by God. Rather, the "invisible attributes" of God are clearly seen and comprehended, stressing two great truths: (1) the fact of the existence of the Godhead or Deity, and (2) the eternal power of that Deity. The apostle's conclusion was that all people are, therefore, without excuse (v. 20).

All people know of God because human beings were created in the image of God (Gen. 1:26–27). The fall of humankind in the Garden of Eden did not erase the image of God but left it severely defaced and scarred. Yet the vestige remained in the form of a conscience.

Being born again leads to a purging or cleansing of the conscience: "How much more, then, will the blood of Christ, who through the eternal Spirit offered himself unblemished to God, cleanse our consciences from acts that lead to death, so that we may serve the living God!" (Heb. 9:14 NIV).

Accepting Jesus as Lord and Savior liberates the conscience to know the will of God: "This is the covenant that I will make with the house of Israel after those days, says the LORD: I will put My laws in their mind and write them on their hearts; and I will be their God, and they shall be My people" (Heb. 8:10 NKJV). God's promise was that the day would come when his people would not need the external Law of Moses to guide them, for the law of God would be written on the heart.

We need to remember that Abraham saw the gospel "in advance": "The Scripture foresaw that God would justify the Gentiles by faith, and announced the gospel in advance to Abraham: 'All nations will be blessed through you'" (Gal. 3:8 NIV). Because of that insight, Abraham perceived the will of God long before God verbalized it in the form of the Ten Commandments. Abraham walked in the Spirit long before the Law told us what righteousness was via those stone tablets. So it was not a stretch for the apostle Paul to write, "But if you are led by the Spirit, you are not under law" (Gal. 5:18 NIV). Being led of the Spirit connects us to the same principle that governed Abraham before the Law came along. This is further evidence of why Paul believed that the Holy Spirit alone is capable of leading us to godly living without the aid of the Law: "The fruit of the Spirit is love, joy, peace, patience, kindness, goodness, faithfulness, gentleness and self-control" (Gal. 5:22–23 NIV). Abraham knew to give a tithe, a tenth, because his faith and knowledge of God may have told him that was what God would want him to do.

WHY SHOULD EVERY CHRISTIAN TITHE?

There is ultimately one reason why every Christian should be a tither: because Jesus said we should. Tithing was so deeply embedded in the Jewish conscience that it needed virtually no mention in the New Testament. Tithing was an assumption in Israel when Jesus came on the scene: "Woe to you, teachers of the law and Pharisees, you hypocrites! You give a tenth of your spices—mint, dill and cummin. But you have neglected the more important matters of the law—justice, mercy and faithfulness. You should have practiced the latter, without neglecting the former" (Matt. 23:23 NIV). If tithing was a part of the Law that would or could be dropped under the new covenant, that was the place our Lord would have done it. He did not.

Tithing teaches us to put God first in our lives, so that we may learn "to revere the LORD [our] God always" (Deut. 14:23 NIV). It reminds us that we owe all we have to God. That God owns it all and allows us to keep the remainder is a testament to his ownership. It was no easier for the people of Israel to tithe than it is for us today. Tithing is an opportunity to test God's promise to provide:

> **"Bring the whole tithe into the storehouse, that there may be food in my house. *Test me in this,*" says the LORD Almighty, "and see if I will not throw open the floodgates of heaven and pour out so much blessing that you will not have room enough for it."** (Mal. 3:10 NIV, emphasis added)

Another reason we should tithe is that Jesus Christ is concerned about the salvation of our souls. And he wants our lives to work while we are on earth. Jesus so thoroughly integrated giving with life that he insisted that only as we learn to give are we learning to live: "Give, and it will be given to you. A good measure, pressed down, shaken together and running over, will be poured into your lap. For with the measure you use, it will be measured to you" (Luke 6:38 NIV).

Tithing works because it changes you. Giving changes the way you view money and possessions. Giving changes your belief that life is about receiving to a new understanding that life is about giving. Giving always guarantees receiving. When you have a spirit of giving, you give not only to God's work but to others as well. Since God is everyone's Source, individuals and opportunities are just channels God uses to bless you and increase your supply. When you give, you can be assured of this: God's resources will work their way back to you in many unexpected and bountiful ways.

Jesus came so that you could reign in life: "For if, by the trespass of the one man, death reigned through that one man, how much more will those who receive God's abundant provision of grace and of the gift of righteousness reign in life through the one man, Jesus Christ" (Rom. 5:17 NIV). He made it abundantly clear that he wants you to have the best that life has to offer: "I have come that they may have life, and have it to the full" (John 10:10 NIV). But to have that good life, you have to give some of what you have received: "Freely you have received, freely give" (Matt. 10:8 NKJV). It seems to be a wonderful law of the universe that happiness and peace of mind become yours when you give to others.

When you start to give in the "spirit of God's release," your material possessions take on a less-significant value. It is a well-documented fact that stress, especially stress related to financial matters, can cause health problems. Most of the stress can be attributed to people worrying about how they are going to pay their bills. But don't you know that when God blesses you, worrying is not part of the deal? "The blessing of the LORD brings wealth, / and he adds no trouble to it" (Prov. 10:22 NIV).

We tend to focus on material blessings when we talk about giving, but the blessing most of us need is to be content with what we have. You see, being rich means having a full supply. In other words, to be rich is to have all our needs met. Many of us need to be released from this "keeping up with the Joneses" mentality. We want more because we think we are falling behind if we don't have what the neighbors have. I am convinced that part of the blessing we receive from giving is that we learn what Paul did:

> **I am not saying this because I am in need, for I have learned to be content whatever the circumstances.** (Phil. 4:11 NIV)

> **Godliness with contentment is great gain.** (1 Tim. 6:6 NIV)

> **Keep your lives free from the love of money and be content with what you have, because God has said,**
> **"Never will I leave you;**
> **never will I forsake you."** (Heb. 13:5 NIV)

THE REWARDS FOR TITHING/GIVING

I want to get personal for a moment. Some of you may be thinking about two questions: *If I give, will there be material blessings in it for me?* and *Are the blessings just spiritual?* God's Word is reassuring:

> *A generous man will prosper;*
> *he who refreshes others will himself be refreshed.*
> (Prov. 11:25 NIV)

> **Seek first the kingdom of God and His righteousness, and all these things shall be added to you.** (Matt. 6:33 NKJV)

> **Anyone who receives instruction in the word must share all good things with his instructor. Do not be deceived: God cannot be mocked. A man reaps what he sows.** (Gal. 6:6–7 NIV)

God aims for us to enjoy life here on earth. He wants us to be powerful witnesses of what he can accomplish through us if we just submit to his will for our lives.

Well, does that mean that you will become rich like Rockefeller or like Bill Gates, the Microsoft founder who is worth more than $40 billion? No, it doesn't mean that. Throughout the book of Proverbs, you find that if you add human giving to God's blessing, you will get your material needs met:

> *Honor the LORD with your wealth,*
> *with the firstfruits of all your crops;*
> *then your barns will be filled to overflowing,*
> *and your vats will brim over with new wine.* (Prov. 3:9–10 NIV)

> *The wicked man earns deceptive wages,*
> *but he who sows righteousness reaps a sure reward.* (Prov. 11:18 NIV)

> *One man gives freely, yet gains even more;*
> *another withholds unduly, but comes to poverty.*
> (Prov. 11:24 NIV)

A generous man will himself be blessed,
  for he shares his food with the poor. (Prov. 22:9
NIV)

Daniel and Jeremiah were two prophets who lived during the period of the Babylonian captivity. Each had a dramatically different economic status.

Daniel was prime minister of the Babylonian Empire. He probably lived in a fine home staffed with servants and earned a nice salary. He must have had the finest "Cadillac chariot."

Daniel was a faithful man of God. He gave us practical and personal help in our Christian walk. He rose to a position of power and prestige in the world system but never compromised essential biblical principles. He showed us how to live a life of spiritual integrity in the crush of a secular world. Anyone who has been tempted to cave in to such pressures will learn much from him.

It is precisely at this point that we identify with Daniel. Regardless of how sheltered our existence has been as children or how often we were taken to Sunday school, there comes a time when we are thrust into a pagan world. We are confronted in a modern university, on the job, or in society with a lifestyle radically different from what is taught in the Bible. At each turn we have to make difficult decisions. Will we obey God regardless of the consequences, or will we become part of the surrounding culture?

Jeremiah, on the other hand, was considered poor. He was repeatedly imprisoned, ridiculed, and impoverished. Yet he also was a faithful man. God called Jeremiah to a painful ministry. But with that great burden he gave Jeremiah a great gift, the gift of himself. From Jeremiah, you will get a glimpse of what it can be like for God and a human being to be together. You will see a message of love that grows from a relationship of love—a hard love, a demanding love, but love nevertheless. You will also discover how you can grow in your personal relationship with God. You will be stronger and more deeply open to the love of God than you were before.

Jeremiah's ministry of faithfulness to God and God's people helped prepare the way for you and me. We can know God in deeper, richer, and more powerful ways because Jeremiah had the courage to be faithful and the wisdom to record his words.

Those two faithful men were at different ends of the economic spectrum. Because of their belief in God, both were persecuted. But they remained faithful and were rewarded. The sovereign majesty of God was evident in the lives of those two men—a God who can predict the future in detail, a God who raises up kings and kingdoms and who also brings them to ruin, a God who can protect Daniel in the lions' den, and a God who is just as concerned about us and our lives.

The faith hall of fame is found in Hebrews 11. Jeremiah and Daniel certainly qualify. It is a record of godly men and women who trusted God when things looked dark or impossible. The author of Hebrews wrote, "These were all commended for their faith, yet none of them received what had been promised. God had planned something better for us so that only together with us would they be made perfect" (11:39–40 NIV).

God in his infinite wisdom and according to his purpose in our lives chooses which of his faithful people he will prosper. But both Daniel and Jeremiah were satisfied with the calling that God had on their lives.

I grew up in the projects of the Bronx. I didn't find out until I went to college that I came from a poor neighborhood. I was satisfied with what I had until I started to compare it with what others had. Most of us are doing better than we think relative to other parts of the world.

In the United States we don't really know what it means to go without. When I say "without," I mean the basics of food, shelter, and clothing. Just the fact that you have the leisure time to read this book puts you in a category that would classify you as wealthy. Many families in the United States own two cars, a house, and nice wardrobes, and they eat every day. Many citizens of developing countries would welcome the opportunity to change places with some of the poor in the United States. To think that God is a genie that we can summon to do our bidding gravely misses the point. The motivation to get a financial blessing—to have our needs met—should not be to get even more, but to obey the Word of God.

No matter what we do for a living, God promises that he will rebuke Satan so that he can't destroy our fruit, which is the blessings that God will give us as a result of our tithes and offerings: "'I will prevent pests from devouring your crops, and the vines in your fields will not cast their fruit,' says the LORD Almighty" (Mal. 3:11 NIV). Now we have authority to overcome Satan: "I have given you authority to trample on snakes and scorpions and to overcome all the power of the enemy; nothing will harm you" (Luke 10:19 NIV). But when it comes to receiving blessings from our tithes and offerings, God says he will make certain that Satan doesn't steal our blessings. This is the only place where God says he will rebuke the devil if he tries to take the blessings from tithing and giving our offerings from us. I am telling you, if you haven't been convinced to tithe after hearing that, then you just don't understand God's Word in regard to giving, and you don't want to be blessed. I don't know about you, but if God can keep Satan at bay, I can get a lot done.

HOW MUCH SHOULD YOU GIVE?

God said, "Bring the whole tithe into the storehouse." Don't hold back any of it. The obedient Israelite didn't ask whether he could give 7 percent instead of 10, or whether he could tithe on the net rather than the gross. Whatever God provided, whether in the form of material or cash or benefits of any sort, 10 percent belonged to God. To help each church member make a personal decision, the Scriptures suggest that giving should be proportionate to one's assets. The Corinthian Christian was taught to bring "a sum of money in keeping with his income" (1 Cor. 16:2 NIV). Macedonian believers "gave as much as they were able, and even beyond their ability" (2 Cor. 8:3 NIV). "According to your means" (2 Cor. 8:11 NIV) or "each according to his ability" (Acts 11:29 NKJV) was the example of the early church. And in the Old Testament, proportionate giving was typical as well.

But to say "proportionate giving" is still a weak answer that leaves much to the option of the giver. Who is the best model? Is the Pharisee who gave "a tenth" the model? "Woe to you, teachers of the law and Pharisees, you hypocrites! You give a tenth of your spices—mint, dill and cummin. But you have neglected the more important matters of the law—justice, mercy and faithfulness. You should have practiced the latter, without neglecting the former" (Matt. 23:23 NIV). Or is Zacchaeus our example in the giving of 50 percent to the poor? "Zacchaeus stood up and said to the Lord, 'Look, Lord! Here and now I give half of my possessions to the poor, and if I have cheated anybody out of anything, I will pay back four times the amount'" (Luke 19:8 NIV). Better yet, is the widow who gave 100 percent the best example of proportionate giving? Jesus "saw a poor widow put in two very small copper coins. 'I tell you the truth,' he said, 'this poor widow has put in more than all the others. All these people gave their gifts out of their wealth; but she out of her poverty put in all she had to live on'" (Luke 21:2–4 NIV).

If we leave the issue up to our own hearts, which are selfish in nature, we might fall short. We need to be weaned from our natural selfishness. How much should the people of God give? It would seem that the answer is twofold. Tithes were paid, and offerings were given.

Three Tithes

However, there were three tithes for the people of Israel. That's right, three. One supported the priests and Levites: "I give to the Levites all the tithes in Israel as their inheritance in return for the work they do while serving at the Tent of Meeting" (Num. 18:21 NIV; see Num. 18:24).

Another provided for a sacred festival:

You must not eat in your own towns the tithe of your grain and new wine and oil, or the firstborn of your herds and flocks, or whatever you have vowed to give, or your freewill offerings or special gifts. Instead, you are to eat them in the presence of the LORD your God at the place the LORD your God will choose—you, your

sons and daughters, your menservants and maidservants, and the Levites from your towns—and you are to rejoice before the LORD your God in everything you put your hand to. (Deut. 12:17–18 NIV; see Deut. 14:23)

The third tithe was for the poor, orphans, and widows: "At the end of every three years, bring all the tithes of that year's produce and store it in your towns, so that the Levites (who have no allotment or inheritance of their own) and the aliens, the fatherless and the widows who live in your towns may come and eat and be satisfied, and so that the LORD your God may bless you in all the work of your hands" (Deut. 14:28–29 NIV; see Deut. 26:12–13).

The first is often called the Levite tithe, the second the festival tithe, and the third the poor tithe. The Levite and festival tithes were ongoing tithes each year, but the poor tithe was taken only every third year. So the three tithes actually amounted to an average of 23 percent per year. Since Israel was not only a spiritual community but a nation, some of the funds were parallel to taxes today. However, they were different from taxes, for people were not penalized for not complying, and the larger portion was for religious, not civic, purposes.

Voluntary Freewill Offerings— Going the Second Mile

The tithe or firstfruits were recognized as belonging to God in the first place. Since the tithe was considered God's, people were not giving a tithe but repaying it to the one to whom it belonged. That is why the Bible speaks of the tithe being "brought" and "presented" or "paid" rather than given. For Israelites, not paying tithes was not an option. They paid tithes out of obedience and duty. But the tithe was only a starting place. They could choose to give additional offerings.

The Old Testament mentions voluntary or "freewill offerings": "And you present to the LORD offerings made by fire, from the herd or the flock, as an aroma pleasing to the LORD— whether burnt offerings or sacrifices, for special vows or freewill offerings or festival offerings" (Num. 15:3 NIV; see Lev. 22:18–23; Deut. 12:6, 17).

Many well-intentioned Christians miss the mark in understanding God's requirement. The Bible asserts that we rob God not only in tithes but in offerings as well: "Will a man rob God? Yet you rob me. But you ask, 'How do we rob you?' In tithes and offerings" (Mal. 3:8 NIV).

Voluntary freewill offerings were contributions beyond the tithe. They constituted perhaps what true giving is all about. People could give as they were led. There was no limit. How had God blessed them? What did they really want to give back to God's kingdom? How much faith did they have that God would supply their needs? Did they really believe that God would "throw open the floodgates of heaven and pour out so much blessing that [they would] not have room enough for it" (Mal. 3:10 NIV)?

When the temple needed to be rebuilt, the people were asked to provide freewill offerings:

> **"The people of any place where survivors may now be living are to provide him with silver and gold, with goods and livestock, and with freewill offerings for the temple of God in Jerusalem." Then the family heads of Judah and Benjamin, and the priests and Levites— everyone whose heart God had moved—prepared to go up and build the house of the LORD in Jerusalem. All their neighbors assisted them with articles of silver and gold, with goods and livestock, and with valuable gifts, in addition to all the freewill offerings.** (Ezra 1:4–6 NIV; see Ezra 3:5; 7:16; 8:28)

If the tithe was a test and demonstration of obedience, then the voluntary offering was a test and demonstration of love, joy, and a heart full of worship for God. In Exodus, we see a tide of generosity among the people because they sensed the greatness of the cause of building the tabernacle. There was a contagious spirit of giving; the people brought more than enough to accomplish the task and had to be restrained from giving:

> [The skilled craftsmen] said to Moses, "The people are
> bringing more than enough for doing the work the
> LORD commanded to be done." Then Moses gave an
> order and they sent this word throughout the camp:
> "No man or woman is to make anything else as an
> offering for the sanctuary." And so the people were
> restrained from bringing more, because what they
> already had was more than enough to do all the work.
> (Ex. 36:5–7 NIV)

Remember what was above and beyond the tithe. Can you imagine how much they had to give before Moses stopped them? To put the situation in the proper context, think for a moment how much the members of your church would have to give before your pastor would ask the congregation to stop giving because they had more than needed to get the Lord's work done.

Another example of God's people going the second mile occurred during the days of David. He said,

> "Besides, in my devotion to the temple of my God I now
> give my personal treasures of gold and silver for the
> temple of my God, over and above everything I have
> provided for this holy temple. . . ." Then the leaders of
> families, the officers of the tribes of Israel, the com-
> manders of thousands and commanders of hundreds,
> and the officials in charge of the king's work gave will-
> ingly. They gave toward the work on the temple of God
> five thousand talents and ten thousand darics of gold,
> ten thousand talents of silver, eighteen thousand talents
> of bronze and a hundred thousand talents of iron. Any
> who had precious stones gave them to the treasury of
> the temple of the LORD in the custody of Jehiel the
> Gershonite. The people rejoiced at the willing response
> of their leaders, for they had given freely and whole-
> heartedly to the LORD. David the king also rejoiced
> greatly. (1 Chron. 29:3, 6–9 NIV)

God's people were very much aware of who the Source of their supply was, who owned it all. David declared,

But who am I, and who are my people, that we should be able to give as generously as this? Everything comes from you, and we have given you only what comes from your hand. . . . O LORD our God, as for all this abundance that we have provided for building you a temple for your Holy Name, it comes from your hand, and all of it belongs to you. I know, my God, that you test the heart and are pleased with integrity. All these things have I given willingly and with honest intent. And now I have seen with joy how willingly your people who are here have given to you. O LORD, God of our fathers Abraham, Isaac and Israel, keep this desire in the hearts of your people forever, and keep their hearts loyal to you. (1 Chron. 29:14, 16–18 NIV)

David measured their loyalty to God by their willingness to give as Jesus recognized Zacchaeus's salvation by his generosity (Luke 19:8–9 NIV).

The disciples "decided" to help the brothers in Judea when they were faced with a famine: "The disciples, *each according to his ability,* decided to provide help for the brothers living in Judea" (Acts 11:29 NIV, emphasis added).

Giving has to be from the heart. You offer the tithe to God because he tells you to give it. When you go the second mile, you go above and beyond in voluntary offerings because having experienced the joys of giving, you want to give even more.

HOW SHOULD WE GIVE?

The term *religiously* has come to describe a disciplined act or consistent regimen. You may hear people say, "He works out religiously," or "She drives the same route to work religiously." You would think that giving in the church would be done religiously. But pastors can tell you that too many people put nothing in the plate when it is passed, and those who give do so sporadically. They may give for several weeks, then miss a week or two. Sometimes they may go several months without giving.

People seldom give when they go out of town or when they are sick. In other words, if they are not in the pew, money doesn't end up in the plate. But if you are out of town when your mortgage or electric bill is due, you still have to pay it. If your giving is an indication of your obedience to God's Word, then why should your giving be haphazard or arbitrary?

The apostle Paul was probably thinking about this hit-and-miss approach when he told the church: "On the first day of every week, each one of you should set aside a sum of money in keeping with his income, saving it up, so that when I come no collections will have to be made" (1 Cor. 16:2 NIV). Systematic, regular giving is basic to biblical giving. If you give the leftovers to God, rather than the firstfruits, you may have little or nothing left over to give.

People aren't likely to give substantially unless they give systematically. By giving systematically $50 a week or several hundred dollars per month, they give substantially more than the person who gives every couple of months or only when she gets a windfall, such as a tax refund or a bonus on the job.

The best way to give is in relation to your income. If you are paid weekly, then give weekly. If you are paid monthly, then give monthly. If you are self-employed and your income varies, then give as often as you receive income.

If you don't set aside the money for God's work, you will rob God by spending it on something else. The great thing about giving immediately upon receiving is that it removes the temptation to rob God.

The church has monthly needs. The church can't pay its employees, utility bills, or other expenses when it feels like it. The budget for the church must be planned, based on the regular giving of its members. If the members give on a regular basis, the church can ensure that it will not only start well, but also finish well in carrying out the work of God.

TO WHOM SHOULD YOU GIVE?

When Christians begin to experience the full Spirit of God, they question many things. They wonder about where they should give their money and how the money should be used: Should I give to my local church or one of those televangelists?

Should I give to some of the organizations that are involved in missions and hunger relief? What about the group that helps homeless people or people with AIDS? How about organizations that address civic, cultural, or community issues? The list is endless.

In the New Testament, giving was to the church, the local Christian assembly. Even gifts that went to other places were distributed through the church. As the Old Testament temple was a storehouse, the New Testament church was a clearinghouse, or better yet a conduit, through which gifts were shared with needy people. No local church can address all the needs of this country or the world. It can do what God has led it to do in the community, but its reach can be greatly extended by helping ministries and missionaries that need its help.

I believe the tithe should go directly to the local church. There is a great deal of room for giving beyond the tithe, some of which can go directly from the believer to worthy ministries and some of which can be channeled to these ministries through the church. The giver's primary spiritual community is the church. The apostle Paul wrote, "Anyone who receives instruction in the word must share all good things with his instructor" (Gal. 6:6 NIV). Paul further called it the minister's "right of support" from the church:

> **This is my defense to those who sit in judgment on me. Don't we have the right to food and drink? Don't we have the right to take a believing wife along with us, as do the other apostles and the Lord's brothers and Cephas? Or is it only I and Barnabas who must work for a living? Who serves as a soldier at his own expense? Who plants a vineyard and does not eat of its grapes? Who tends a flock and does not drink of the milk? Do I say this merely from a human point of view? Doesn't the Law say the same thing? For it is written in the Law of Moses: "Do not muzzle an ox while it is treading out the grain." Is it about oxen that God is concerned? Surely he says this for us, doesn't he? Yes, this was written for us, because when the plowman plows and the thresher threshes, they ought to do so in**

the hope of sharing in the harvest. If we have sown spiritual seed among you, is it too much if we reap a material harvest from you? If others have this right of support from you, shouldn't we have it all the more? But we did not use this right. On the contrary, we put up with anything rather than hinder the gospel of Christ. (1 Cor. 9:3–12 NIV)

He summed up his position by saying, "Don't you know that those who work in the temple get their food from the temple, and those who serve at the altar share in what is offered on the altar? In the same way, the Lord has commanded that those who preach the gospel should receive their living from the gospel" (1 Cor. 9:13–14 NIV).

Paul felt that the faithful church minister and missionary should be paid, and paid very well. Being paid more than they need gives them the opportunity to live as examples to congregations. Many Christians believe that pastors should live on salaries that are slightly above poverty wages. But that is not God's way: "The elders who direct the affairs of the church well are worthy of double honor, especially those whose work is preaching and teaching. For the Scripture says, 'Do not muzzle the ox while it is treading out the grain,' and 'The worker deserves his wages'" (1 Tim. 5:17–18 NIV).

Paul didn't encourage believers to give to a needy cause on their own; rather, he felt that they should consolidate their funds and give to and through the local church: "On the first day of every week, each one of you should set aside a sum of money in keeping with his income, saving it up, so that when I come no collections will have to be made" (1 Cor. 16:2 NIV).

Many of the first Christians sold property and let the spiritual leaders distribute funds to those in need: "There were no needy persons among them. For from time to time those who owned lands or houses sold them, brought the money from the sales and put it at the apostles' feet, and it was distributed to anyone as he had need" (Acts 4:34–35 NIV). The early Christians did not decide where the money was to go. The funds were given, and spiritually qualified leaders distributed the money using their collective wisdom, knowledge, and leading from God.

In Old Testament times, one might give above and beyond the tithe and offerings to the needs of an individual, yet basic giving to God was to a centralized location. That location was the temple, for distribution by the Levites. In New Testament times, the local church—not the building, mind you, but the body of Christ—was the center for distribution by the spiritual leaders.

By supporting an individual church, then, you support the ministry of that church and provide funds for that church to in turn send the gospel around the world. Through your tithes and offerings, you can preach the gospel in India, teach a Bible class in Africa, help the sick in a hospital in the United States, translate the Bible into the language of the Indonesians, or love an orphaned child in Korea. Giving to your local church helps fulfill the Great Commission: "Therefore go and make disciples of all nations, baptizing them in the name of the Father and of the Son and of the Holy Spirit, and teaching them to obey everything I have commanded you. And surely I am with you always, to the very end of the age" (Matt. 28:19–20 NIV).

Well, what happens if you don't agree with the way the money is spent? As a former finance committee chairman at my local church, I can honestly say that the church leaders are in a much better position to judge where the money should go. Nevertheless, there should be an overall vision for your church, and the money being spent should support that vision. I encourage anyone who has concerns to discuss the matter with the pastor and/or church leaders. It is important that you take this action rather than quietly give your money to another organization or church without confronting the issue.

Some Christians try to exert too much control over the funds that they give to their local church. The Bible says we should pay our taxes: "Give everyone what you owe him: If you owe taxes, pay taxes; if revenue, then revenue; if respect, then respect; if honor, then honor" (Rom. 13:7 NIV). We do this knowing that some of the money will be wasted and go toward purposes with which we would not agree. I am concerned that we are overly critical about every dollar we give the church, but we do not raise concerns with our local and national political leaders about how our tax dollars are spent.

Once you have had a chance to discuss the matter with your church leaders, yet you still cannot freely give to your church, it may be time for you to ask God to help you find a church where you can give obediently and wholeheartedly. Churches are under God's direction, but they are run by imperfect people. The grass may always seem greener on the other side. I don't encourage Christians to move from church to church, but to continue attending a church that you fail to support with your tithes and offerings is not biblically acceptable.

Give your tithe to your local church, and direct your offerings elsewhere if you desire. But make sure there are not additional needs identified by your church that can use your support. With your offerings you can support a wide range of organizations that minister to the need that God has placed on your heart. Check out these organizations carefully. With your local church, at least you have the opportunity to witness firsthand the character and integrity of the church leaders. For an organization that may or may not be local, determining this is difficult. All you may know about the ministry is what it tells you through the mail or on radio or television. If possible, get involved as a volunteer in these organizations so that you can get comfortable sending them money.

Our giving is a response to the call of discipleship. Are we willing to follow in the steps of Jesus Christ? If giving is a reflection of how close we are to God, our giving results in reciprocating God's grace. But keep in mind that we still can't beat God in the giving department, for he gave us the unmatchable gift. He sent his Son, Jesus, to make the ultimate sacrifice. Jesus left the riches of heaven to deliver us from eternal death and grant us eternal riches.

— 5 —

SAVING AND INVESTING

MOTIVES FOR SAVING

The number one prerequisite for saving and investing is attitude. I believe that any motivation for investing that excludes God's will for our lives will not be blessed. The basic question you must ask is, Why do I want to invest? There are two reasons to save and invest your money. *The first reason is to advance the kingdom of God* by making some of the profits from your investment activities available for ministry.

Our basic mission as followers of Christ is to spread the gospel, and we all know that takes money. Investing our money is one way to be good stewards over what God has entrusted to us, and we may gain additional resources to finance kingdom work.

One of the more popular parables of Jesus highlighted investing. The parable of the talents told about a master who tested the attitude and faithfulness of investors in his absence (Matt. 25:14–30). Today, the largest amount mentioned, five talents, would be equivalent to more than $1 million, and the smallest amount, one talent, would be $222,000. If Jesus didn't approve of investing, why would he use it as an example and reward the individuals who were most diligent and responsible? Investing is just an extension of good stewardship. God calls us to take some risks to multiply what he has entrusted to us.

Some people have the gift of giving: "We have different gifts, according to the grace given us. . . . If it is contributing to the needs of others, let him give generously; if it is leadership, let him govern diligently; if it is showing mercy, let him do it cheerfully" (Rom. 12:6, 8 NIV). To these individuals, the multiplication of material worth is an extension of their basic ministry. They have a gift and/or talent that allows them to earn much more than average workers. But the gift of giving allows them to cheerfully give to God's work far above their tithes and offerings.

The second reason to invest is to take care of your family: "If anyone does not provide for his relatives, and especially for his immediate family, he has denied the faith and is worse than an unbeliever" (1 Tim. 5:8 NIV). This biblical truth would encompass making sure that the family's basic needs are met in the form of food, clothing, and housing. It would also be prudent to extend this list to include saving and investing to allow children to attend college, planning for retirement, and perhaps starting a business.

The key test when it comes to investing is your motivation. Sometimes the answer is not so obvious. You already know that God encourages saving (Prov. 21:20 NIV), but he detests hoarding:

> **Then he said, "This is what I'll do. I will tear down my barns and build bigger ones, and there I will store all my grain and my goods. And I'll say to myself, 'You have plenty of good things laid up for many years. Take life easy; eat, drink and be merry.'" But God said to him, "You fool! This very night your life will be demanded from you. Then who will get what you have prepared for yourself?" This is how it will be with anyone who stores up things for himself but is not rich toward God.** (Luke 12:18–21 NIV)

You must continually search your heart to make sure that your motives are pure, that you have not become greedy by longing to have more and more or bigger and better: "For of this you can be sure: No immoral, impure or greedy person—such a man is an idolater—has any inheritance in the kingdom of Christ and of God" (Eph. 5:5 NIV).

So when do you know enough is enough? Many verses deal with material riches. But God's Word doesn't say that poverty is the alternative. As a matter of fact, the biblical standard seems to be something in the middle: "I know what it is to be in need, and I know what it is to have plenty. I have learned the secret of being content in any and every situation, whether well fed or hungry, whether living in plenty or in want" (Phil. 4:12 NIV). God wants you to understand that money is a tool to use in accomplishing his plans through you. If you are to be happy with what God has given you, then you need guidelines.

Seek God's will for your life. Jesus said, "Seek first the kingdom of God and His righteousness, and all these things shall be added to you" (Matt. 6:33 NKJV). If God is not first in your life, any success you have will be short-lived, and you will never be truly happy. Knowing what God would have you do with your life gives your possessions a different meaning. No longer will you be trying to accumulate things, but you will be more interested in how to use the things to serve God by making more disciples.

Pursue a reasonable standard of living. There is not a "one size fits all" standard of living that a single person or married couple need to adopt. God has placed Christians at every financial lifestyle imaginable. No matter what your economic scenario, God has a plan for your life. Remember, just having an abundance is not a sign of God's blessings. Satan can easily duplicate worldly riches. Through prayer, God will reveal to you what your financial lifestyle should be. Every purchase decision should become captive to the will of God. But no matter where God leads you in your decision in this area, the key is to be happy and content with his provision for you: "I am not saying this because I am in need, for I have learned to be content whatever the circumstances" (Phil. 4:11 NIV); and "Keep your lives free from the love of money and be content with what you have, because God has said, 'Never will I leave you; / never will I forsake you'" (Heb. 13:5 NIV).

Give. Nothing guards your heart better against coveting and greed than giving. Tithing and submitting offerings to God help you remember that you are only a steward. God is the owner, and as a manager, you must take proper care of God's resources and use them for his purposes. The question you might want to keep in the back of your mind when trying to determine whether you are coveting a particular item is, How would I feel if I lost it or perhaps it was taken away from me? If you think you are getting attached to a material possession, give it away or let someone borrow it. Believe me, the blessings will come back to you in marvelous and magnificent ways.

Set priorities. Too often Christians have fallen on hard times because they have not set firm priorities to rule their decisions regarding time, talent, and resources (money and the things money can buy). Financial decisions are filtered through the world's values instead of God's will for their lives. They become more obsessed with how the world views their decisions than with how God sees them. God's Word says that we have been given both responsibility and authority on this earth. We are to plan our way, and God will provide the direction: "In his heart a man plans his course, / but the LORD determines his steps" (Prov. 16:9 NIV).

No one has perfect insight into God's will for him or her. It's a day-by-day process. But God promises you guidance to keep you on track if you are willing to listen and step out in faith: "I say to you, if you have faith as a mustard seed, you will say to this mountain, 'Move from here to there,' and it will move; and nothing will be impossible for you" (Matt. 17:20 NKJV).

HOW TO SAVE

How much do you save on a regular basis? Some people don't save anything. It's not that they don't want to save; the reason lies closer to not knowing how and in what amounts to save. A good rule of thumb is to save 10 percent of your monthly net income. But if you can't handle 10 percent, why not start with 2 or 5 percent? You should start now and be consistent. The earlier you start saving, the better. (See fig. 6.)

Many Christians would be hard-pressed to save 10 percent of their income, but the biblical standard is closer to 20 percent. In Genesis is the story of Joseph and Pharaoh's dream:

Then Joseph said to Pharaoh, "The dreams of Pharaoh are one and the same. God has revealed to Pharaoh what he is about to do. The seven good cows are seven years, and the seven good heads of grain are seven years; it is one and the same dream. The seven lean, ugly cows that came up afterward are seven years, and so are the seven worthless heads of grain scorched by the east wind: They are seven years of famine." (Gen. 41:25–27 NIV)

Joseph devised a careful savings plan in light of the famine he predicted would be coming upon Egypt: "Let Pharaoh appoint commissioners over the land to take a fifth of the harvest of Egypt during the seven years of abundance. They should collect all the food of these good years that are coming and store up the grain under the authority of Pharaoh, to be kept in the cities for food" (Gen. 41:34–35 NIV). Every year for seven years a large portion (one-fifth, or 20 percent) of the harvest was stored. Then when the seven years of famine came, they used the stores of grain to meet their current needs. Not only did they have grain for their country, but their abundance was such that they were able to sell grain to other countries.

In today's economy the seven years of famine would represent a depression, and the seven years of plenty would translate into low inflation, a rising stock market, and a booming economy. During those years of prosperity, it would be wise to save and invest 20 percent of your income. Then when the depression came, you would have ample savings to weather the storm.

To put this biblical story in proper perspective, consider this: suppose you saved 20 percent of your income from the time you received your first paycheck. How much money do you think you would have? A lot, right? Furthermore, since you are giving 10 percent to the Lord, having the discipline to save at least 20 percent of your income would mean that you would have to live on the remaining 70 percent. Living on 70 percent of your income would no doubt affect every financial decision from what kind of car you drive to the kind of house or apartment you live in to clothes you wear.

The more you save, the easier it becomes, and the faster you'll meet your goals. For instance, if your monthly gross income is $1,000 and you save just 10 percent, that will equal $100 each month, or $1,200 per year plus interest. Now, saving requires you to use discipline, but you can do it. *Your future depends on it.*

Saving money is like having insurance. You don't realize it's important until you need it. The first type of savings plan that comes to mind is making a regular deposit to your savings account. Many people have found it much easier to save by pay-roll deduction—having the employer deduct a fixed amount from the paycheck each pay period and applying it to a desig-nated savings vehicle. This method gets the money out of your hands before you spend it. If your employer doesn't have a pay-roll deduction plan, many banks will draft your checking account each month and deposit it in a savings account. But if you want to write a check to deposit in your savings account, make sure it is the first check you write when you sit down to pay your bills. The savings habit is its own reward.

A CASH RESERVE

Saving money consistently will prepare you for investing. A cash reserve is the foundation of any financial plan (see fig. 7). The main benefit of your cash reserve is that you earn a safe and guaranteed return and the funds can be converted to cash without a penalty or loss of principal. Your total cash reserve should be equal to at least six months' expenses. If your monthly expenses total $1,000, your cash reserve should amount to at least $6,000.

Why do you need a cash reserve? It gives you an immediate supply of hard cash to cover monthly expenses in the event of an emergency. The money to build your cash reserve will come from your regular savings plan. That's the 5 or 10 percent of your monthly net income you promised to set aside on a regular basis. A cash reserve will protect you from financial hardship.

TYPES OF SAVINGS ACCOUNTS

What type of savings account is best for you? Consult a knowledgeable bank representative or financial consultant. By outlining your investment objectives and seeking advice, you can more clearly see your alternatives, and you can make choices. Your investment objectives for your six-month cash reserve must be safe and easily converted to cash. For starters, you will need a money market account, which will allow you to make deposits and withdrawals without a penalty. Keep the equivalent of three months' expenses in this account.

A certificate of deposit, commonly called a CD, is a redeemable bond issued by a bank with a maturity of from ninety days to five years. If the interest rate is high, you can keep an amount equal to three months' expenses in this type of account with a maturity of not more than three months.

So you will have a total of six months' expenses all in one money market account or divided equally between a money market account and a CD. A savings account and a CD are important tools for building your cash reserve fund.

COMPOUND VERSUS SIMPLE INTEREST

Benjamin Franklin wrote, "Money can earn money, and its offspring can earn more." Once you start comparing savings accounts, you'll discover that the interest rate can be calculated several ways. The interest rate you receive on your money is as significant as how often the interest is compounded.

Compound interest is the method by which your interest earns interest. Simple interest means you don't receive interest on your interest; you earn interest only on the principal, the original amount you deposited.

For example, $1,000 compounded monthly at 9 percent will grow to $1,309 in three years. The same amount at 9 percent simple interest will grow to only $1,270, a difference of almost $40. The advantage of compound interest is even more evident with larger amounts. It is equally important for you to know how often your interest is being compounded—yearly, quarterly, monthly, or daily. Don't be afraid to ask questions about your money. Learn all the details.

INVESTING YOUR MONEY

Are you a saver or an investor? There is a difference.

A saver tries to preserve and keep the money safe. A saver looks for guaranteed financial vehicles. He is more concerned with getting his original investment back. He wants to be sure that when he wants his money, it will be there.

An investor puts the money at risk to achieve a higher financial return. An investor commits money to an investment where the return is not guaranteed or very safe. When it is time to cash in the investment, the investor may receive more or less than she put in. The investor realizes that what she gives up in safety, she may get back many times in higher returns.

People with financial savvy save a certain amount of money toward their cash reserve fund and invest a separate amount for their investment fund.

Building an Investment Fund

Beginning an investment fund is the key to building wealth (see fig. 7). Once you have enough in your savings to pay all your bills and expenses for six months, you have satisfied the requirements of your cash reserve, and it's time to start your investment fund. Some people ask me, "I have $500. Where should I invest the money?" My response is always the same. Until you have satisfied your cash reserve goal, investing should not be an option. Here's why.

When you start to invest, you will be selecting vehicles whose principal will fluctuate in value. If you invest money that you may need for an emergency later on, then chances are, you may have to sell at a time when the value of the investment is down. Consequently you will lose money. The money for your investment fund will come from your regular savings pledge and any excess you have accumulated in your cash reserve fund.

The goal for your investment fund will be to earn higher yields than could be attained through a regular savings account.

In addition, you must be willing to accept a slightly higher degree of risk in exchange for a higher return.

Money invested will be divided into two categories—appreciation and income. Appreciation or growth investments include growth stocks and real estate. Income investments are centered mostly on different types of bonds and some stocks.

Risk and Return

The return on your investment should outweigh the risk. If you are prepared to accept greater risk, you may achieve even higher returns on your investments. The relationship between risk and return does not mean that you will always earn higher returns on your investments by taking greater risks. But if there is a high degree of risk, you should expect a higher return.

Risk involves the possibility of loss. All investments have some degree of risk. Risk focuses on the future and the ability to forecast results based on past experiences. A basic rule of investing is never to invest more than you can afford to lose. Persons who are risk takers in life tend to go for the higher risks in their investments.

Investment Tips

Don't fall for get-rich-quick schemes. From Proverbs, we learn that "a faithful man will be richly blessed, / but one eager to get rich will not go unpunished" (Prov. 28:20 NIV). Get-rich-quick schemes sound great on the surface. They usually offer an exorbitant gain with little or no apparent risk. So how can a Christian avoid the traps of get-rich-quick scam artists? Here are some tips:

• Don't make emotional decisions. Avoid making decisions based on your *emotional* response to an offer. Most promoters of these deals will use your desire to become a success, eliminate or avoid income taxes, and/or secure your family's future as a lure to push you to avoid good judgment when making a decision. God's Word advises:

> *Do not wear yourself out to get rich;*
> *have the wisdom to show restraint.*
> *Cast but a glance at riches, and they are gone,*
> *for they will surely sprout wings*
> *and fly off to the sky like an eagle.* (Prov. 23:4–5
> NIV)

• Get advice from a Christian friend or adviser. Before deciding to pursue a particular get-rich-quick deal, ask a trusted adviser or friend to look it over. Better yet, if there is an introductory meeting, take your friend along. Someone who is not attached to the deal is more likely to spot potential problems and pitfalls. Keep your mind open to the advice the person shares: "The way of a fool seems right to him, / but a wise man listens to advice" (Prov. 12:15 NIV).

Diversify No one is right all the time. Even when you think you can't lose, never put all your eggs in one basket:

> *Cast your bread upon the waters,*
> *for after many days you will find it again.*
> *Give portions to seven, yes to eight,*
> *for you do not know what disaster may come upon*
> *the land.* (Eccl. 11:1–2 NIV)

Diversifying allows you to spread your risk by realizing that not all investments go up at the same time. By spreading the risk, you are taking advantage of the reality that there is a season for every type of investment. For example, generally stocks rise in value in a low-inflation and low–interest rate environment. On the other hand, real estate rises in value in inflationary times.

You never really know how your investments will pan out until you are ready to sell them. In addition, no one can predict the future, including investment analysts who show up on the numerous financial shows. Evaluate each investment opportunity carefully, then allocate your money among various options. For stocks, this means having at least ten to fifteen in your portfolio, covering several key industries. If you are investing in mutual funds, then you need at least five different funds with various investment objectives. (I will discuss mutual funds and stocks in detail later.)

Invest in what you know. Scamming someone in an area in which the person has expertise is unusual. If you are a computer expert, seldom would a get-rich-quick offer in that field dupe you. Many times I have heard from individuals who are considering an investment that they don't understand. I tell them to get more information so that they understand the offer or don't do it. We all do well to heed this advice: "By wisdom a house is built, / and through understanding it is established" (Prov. 24:3 NIV).

BONDS

A bond is an IOU, or promissory note. When you buy a bond, the issuer promises to repay the principal you have loaned him or her on a specific date. In the meantime, interest is paid twice a year at a fixed annual rate set when the bonds were first offered for sale.

Bondholders have first access to the company's assets in case of bankruptcy because the assets usually serve as collateral for the bonds. This policy makes bonds a much safer investment than stocks. However, bondholders are not owners of the company and will not participate in increased earnings or in the growth of the company.

Bond-rating agencies, such as Moody's and Standard & Poor's, judge the creditworthiness of companies issuing the bonds. This evaluation is similar to a credit check made by a bank for a consumer loan. Companies with the best ratings can issue bonds at lower interest rates.

Should You Invest in Bonds?

Bonds have been the traditional counterpart to common stocks in a balanced investment portfolio. Bonds have advantages and disadvantages.

On the positive side, the interest rate on a bond is fixed and is paid twice a year. And if you buy municipal bonds, the interest is free of federal and sometimes state income taxes. The principal on your bonds will be repaid at a set maturity date. You can even use bonds as collateral for a loan.

On the negative side, the market value of your bonds can fluctuate with changes in interest rates. The interest rate on bonds is fixed and will not change over the years. An interest rate that looks attractive now may not be so in later years.

Municipal Bonds

You can save money on your taxes by investing in municipal bonds, which are issued by local governments, counties, cities, and states. Munis, as they are often referred to as, offer interest free of federal income tax. Most states also allow the income to be exempt from state and local taxes if the bonds are issued locally.

The after-tax yield on municipal bonds may be even greater than the yield on taxable investments, such as savings accounts. Here's how this works: a municipal bond that pays interest at 7 percent is equivalent to the return of an investor in the 28 percent tax bracket earning almost 10 percent on a taxable investment.

Buying municipal bonds can help you achieve better after-tax yields. The simple calculation in the worksheet (see fig. 8) will tell you what taxable return you would have to earn to equal the tax-free return of a municipal bond. Use the calculation to compare taxable and tax-free yields based on your tax situation. Remember, it's not what you earn that's important; it's what you get to keep.

Corporate Bonds

Corporate bonds offer not only generous yields but price stability as well. Corporations issue bonds to finance various projects. The two major types of corporate bonds are mortgage obligations and debentures.

Mortgage obligation bonds are backed by a lien on property—a factory, a power plant, or an airplane. Debentures, on the other hand, are guaranteed only by the promise of the company to repay the money and are not backed by any specific assets.

To help investors judge the financial soundness of a company, corporate bonds are given ratings that range from D to AAA (the highest) by Moody's and Standard & Poor's. These ratings measure the safety of interest and principal payments and are not to be used as recommendations to buy or sell.

Government Bonds

If safety is your primary investment objective, government bonds are the best investment for you. These bonds are the responsibility of the U.S. government, which guarantees their principal and interest. You can purchase government bonds at your local bank or through your regional Federal Reserve Bank office.

Series EE bonds are sold at a discount from face value, and they pay full value at maturity. Series HH bonds earn interest twice a year. They are purchased at face value, and they are available only through conversion of Series EE bonds.

There are three basic types of Treasury securities. Treasury bills are issued at a discount from face value with maturities of ninety-one days to one year, with a minimum investment of $10,000. Treasury notes have a fixed maturity of one to ten years and pay interest twice a year. Treasury bonds are similar to Treasury notes but have maturities of more than ten years and higher yields. Notes and bonds require a $1,000 minimum investment.

Zero Coupon Bonds

Zero coupon bonds may be your ticket to a comfortable retirement for you or a college education for the kids. They have become one of the more popular investment products introduced in recent years.

The term *zero coupon* is used because the interest has been separated from the principal on these bonds, and there are no coupons to clip. With regular bonds, you periodically detach coupons to obtain interest from them.

You buy zero coupon bonds at a deep discount—anywhere from 20 to 90 percent of their face value. You receive the full face value of the bonds at maturity. The return is the difference between the price you pay for the bonds and the face value. The interest accrues each year, but you receive it only at maturity.

Advantages of zeros. Several advantages have made zero coupon bonds popular investments. They offer convenience;

you don't have to remember to clip coupons to receive your interest. You don't have to worry about reinvesting the interest income as it accrues. In addition, you know from the outset what return the investment will provide and how much you will receive at maturity.

Zero coupon bonds also provide you with much-needed flexibility for investment planning. You can select a maturity date for a zero that will meet the specific cash needs you anticipate, whether six months or thirty years down the road, such as a second home, retirement, or a college education for your children.

Types of zeros. Zero coupon bonds come in a variety of forms. Treasury-backed zeros provide excellent security since they represent obligations of the U.S. Treasury. Corporations and municipal governments also issue zeros. Tax-exempt municipal bond zeros are gaining in popularity and may provide a good choice for high-tax-bracket investors. Zero coupon municipal bonds may offer investors a better way to reach their objectives than with traditional tax-free, fixed-income investments.

Imagine you need $100,000 in twenty-five years when you retire. Simply invest $20,000 in zero coupon bonds, maturing at that time, selling at about $200 each. In this example, your capital gain would be equal to five times your original investment.

When interest rates are falling, the price (how much you paid) of your bond will rise; when interest rates are rising, the price of your bond will fall.

WALL STREET TALK

Traders on Wall Street, like people in any profession, have their own jargon, a specialized vocabulary that gives new meaning to certain words.

Take the terms *bear* and *bull markets*. Bear is shorthand for pessimism or a decline in growth. Bull refers to optimism or growth in the economy. A person who is bullish believes securities prices will rise. A bear thinks prices will fall. Bear markets often follow bad economic news.

If you play the Wall Street game, you need not be one way or the other. You can be bullish on stocks in general but bearish on steel stocks. To determine what investments to make, you would be wise to first decide in which direction the economy is moving, bullish (which is up) or bearish (which is down).

What Is a Load?

Mutual funds are separated into two groups—load funds and no-load funds. Loads are the sales fees charged by the fund and paid to the broker or financial planner who sells you the shares in the fund. (The two types of mutual funds are discussed later in this chapter.)

What Is the Dow?

The Dow is the nickname for the Dow Jones Industrial Average of thirty major stocks. The list includes companies such as IBM, Exxon, and McDonald's. The Dow is the most widely quoted economic measurement. It is believed to be a symbol of the rise and fall of stock prices, and it offers an indication of how the economy is doing in general.

Knowing how much the Dow goes up or down on any given day is less important than knowing the trend. You can use the Dow as an aid in evaluating your stock's performance. If the Dow rose 20 percent one year and your stock rose only 10 percent, you know your stock underperformed the market. You may want to consider selling your stock, changing your broker, or revising your investment strategy.

Buying Stocks Over the Counter

There are more than 1,600 stocks listed on the New York Stock Exchange, and more than 1,100 on the American Stock Exchange. These numbers are dwarfed by the 20,000 or more stocks listed on the over-the-counter market, or OTC.

The primary OTC market is known as the National Association of Securities Dealers Automated Quotations, or NASDAQ. This system offers a computer and telephone communications network that connects brokers who represent buyers and sellers all over the country. This system is so efficient, it rivals the New York Stock Exchange in importance.

Many major companies choose to sell their securities over the counter. The phrase "OTC market" refers to the time when some stocks had to be purchased at the offices of brokers or banks, literally over the counter.

OWNING A PIECE OF AMERICA

By buying and selling stock, you can own part of America. The purchase or sale of stock is really a simple process. However, you will have to enlist the help of a stockbroker to complete the transaction.

After you place your order with your broker, if it's a stock on the New York Stock Exchange, the broker wires it to the exchange. The price is then negotiated and relayed back to your broker for confirmation.

Brokers charge a fee or commission to handle the transaction. The fee is determined by the number of shares you are buying and the price of the stock.

Stocks are usually bought and sold in groups of one hundred, called round lots. You can buy three or four shares, but the price may be higher. Stock bought in an amount less than one hundred is called an odd lot.

STOCKS

In general, a business is organized as a sole proprietorship, a partnership, or a corporation. But only corporations are allowed to issue stocks and bonds.

A corporation is a legal entity apart from its owners, the shareholders. It can own property in its own name, incur debts, and sue and be sued. This separate existence means that shareholders are in a position of limited liability.

If the corporation can't pay its debts, no shareholder has to assume the debts. The corporation can simply declare bankruptcy. But in a partnership or sole proprietorship, the personal assets of the owners can be taken and used to satisfy any debt that the company incurs.

All corporations have stock. One type is called common; the other type is called preferred.

Common Stock

When you own common stock, you have certain rights as a shareholder in a corporation: the right to vote and elect directors of the company, the right to receive your share of profits in the form of dividends, and the right to receive a copy of the corporation's annual report.

As a common stockholder, you don't have first claim on the assets and earnings of the company. That privilege is reserved for creditors, bondholders, and preferred stockholders.

Common stock offers you the best possibility of growth, and it is considered to be a hedge against inflation. Investing in common stocks offers you an excellent opportunity to participate in the growth of a company and the nation's economy but is riskier than investing in preferred stocks or bonds.

Preferred Stock

Does *preferred* mean "better"? It doesn't necessarily. The word *preferred* relates to having priority over the common stockholders when it comes to the distribution of dividends and assets in the event of the breakup of a corporation.

Preferred stock is a cross between stocks and bonds. The dividend yield is fixed and limited, and preferred stock has no maturity. Shareholders with this type of stock are considered owners of the corporation, just like common shareholders, but preferred shareholders generally don't have voting rights.

Many investors buy preferred stock for the steady income it offers and the hope that their principal will increase over the years. Although growth possibilities with preferred stock are not as good as with common stock, preferred stock is usually an appropriate vehicle for protecting your original investment, except during severe inflationary periods.

Why Invest in Stocks?

Historically stocks have been one of the top investments. The Center for Research in Security Prices at the University of

Chicago has conducted studies on stock market prices since 1926. One of the most significant findings disclosed that if an investor had chosen any stock at random, and had bought and sold that stock at random over a period from 1926 to 1960, the person would have made a profit 78 percent of the time.

The average return on the investment, assuming the person reinvested all dividends paid on the stock, would have been 9.8 percent a year. These are considered spectacular findings since Americans went through a depression and a major world war during that time period.

Even though the economic outlook may seem uncertain, the potential for above-average returns will always remain in the stock market.

Profits in Stocks

How do you know a stock with real growth potential when you see one? Compared to bonds, which are designed to pay a fixed amount of interest, the return on a common stock investment can be hard to predict. However, many useful methods estimate what kind of return a stock is likely to produce. These methods draw on a wide range of information, including economic data, the interest rate outlook, industry trends, and world events. Equally important, stock selection requires a close look at a corporation's financial history, its current business, and its prospects for the future. All of the information you need to properly analyze a stock is available from government sources or directly from the company. Most can also be found at your public library.

When buying stocks, most investors turn to the ratings and recommendations compiled by analysts at investment firms and investment publications.

How the Economy Affects Stocks

An ironic fact is that a rapidly growing economy can be bad for stocks. The level of growth expected for the economy and interest-rate forecasts influence the outlook for stock performance. In a growing economy—measured by such indicators as new housing starts, retail sales, and industrial production—

corporate profits often rise. These increased profits, or expected increases in profits, can push stock prices up.

If the economy grows too quickly and "overheats," demand for money to fund expansion can shoot up and produce higher interest rates. These higher rates reduce corporate profits because of the higher cost of borrowing. In addition, higher interest rates can drive investors away from stocks and into money markets and other fixed-income investments.

In Which Industries Should You Buy Stocks?

You should consider three broad categories of industry groups.

Defensive industries tend to offer stability, weathering poor economic conditions better than other types of industries. Food and drug companies and utilities fall into this category.

Cyclical industries, unlike defensive industries, tend to fare poorly during economic downturns but blossom with an expanding economy. Companies in the steel, automotive, paper, and housing industries are good examples.

Growth industries are expanding, typically because of a growing demand for goods or services produced by the industries. Examples today include robotics, health care, and computer services. Companies in growth industries provide stockholders with greater potential for profit.

Rating the Performance of a Stock

A stock analyst devotes a large segment of time to looking at the past, present, and future performance of individual companies and their stock.

As a stockholder, you can collect profits through dividend payments, growth in the value of your stock, or both. There are two ways of measuring your return—the dividend yield and the earnings yield.

The dividend yield is obtained by dividing the dividend payout by the price of the stock. Instead of paying dividends, some companies plow all earnings back into operations. This method increases the companies' profits and, they hope, the stock price. Because of this, additional measures are used to size up stocks.

The earnings yield, determined by dividing the stock price by earnings, shows what a company is earning in relation to the price of the stock.

This same basic information is sometimes called the price/earnings ratio, or multiple. For example, a company may earn $2 per share and sell at $30 per share. The price/earnings ratio (P/E as it is sometimes referred to) is fifteen, that is, thirty divided by two.

A high P/E ratio shows investor enthusiasm in the prospects for the stock. A low P/E ratio may mean that the stock has been spurned by investors or that the stock's potential is not widely recognized.

This approach to stock evaluation is called fundamental analysis. It includes an evaluation of a company's assets, profits, management, and products.

DIVIDEND REINVESTMENT PLANS

Looking for ways to invest in the stock market? How would you like to invest in solid Fortune 500 companies conveniently and inexpensively? Dividend reinvestment plans (DRIPs) may just fill the bill.

As the name indicates, dividend reinvestment plans allow you to reinvest your dividends automatically in additional shares in the company. The advantages of this plan include not paying any brokerage commissions and not needing a lot of money to get started. If the company has a stock purchase plan, you may also be able to purchase stock directly from the company, often at a reduced cost.

To get started, you must purchase one share of stock from a stockbroker, then have the stock registered in your name and mailed to you. When you receive the stock certificate, request information on the company's dividend reinvestment plan. A list of more than seven hundred firms that offer reinvestment plans is available from the Standard & Poor's Corporation (25 Broadway, New York, NY 10004). Also newsletters offer directories of these plans: *The MoneyPaper* (1010 Mamaroneck Avenue, Mamaroneck, NY 10543; 914-381-5400) and *The DRIP Investor* (7412 Calumet Avenue, Hammond, IN 46324-2692; 219-931-6480). Or you can call your local stockbroker for more information.

MUTUAL FUNDS

Investing in mutual funds can be a safe and convenient way to invest in stocks or bonds. A mutual fund is a type of investment group set up to invest for a specific purpose. Basically here's how a mutual fund works: a number of investors pool their money, determine an investment objective, and invest the money in a group of stocks or bonds to achieve that objective.

They may invest in securities designed to achieve growth, income, or both. Each investor in the fund receives a certain amount of shares in proportion to the money invested. The day-to-day value of the shares is calculated by dividing the total value of the securities by the number of shares outstanding on that day. The resulting figure is called the net asset value. The net asset value will go up or down depending on whether the stocks or bonds in the fund rise or fall.

Why Invest in a Mutual Fund?

The main reason to invest is that you can make money with mutual funds. The average growth fund has averaged at least 12 percent a year. But some funds have gained as much as 50 percent in one year. Not bad! Also, mutual funds can be bought for small or large amounts of money. Some funds will accept an initial investment of only $250. Investors like mutual funds because they offer diversification and the opportunity to invest in a fund that suits almost any investment objective.

Funds offer professional management for people who want to invest in the stock market but are too busy to manage their money on a day-to-day basis. You can easily get your money out of a fund or exchange it with other funds. Mutual funds are a smart investment for retirement plans.

How to Select a Mutual Fund

You may choose from thousands of mutual funds. The first step in selecting a mutual fund is to define your investment objectives for the next five years or more. Are you looking for growth, income, or just a parking place for extra cash?

Talk with a stockbroker or consult such sources as *Forbes* magazine's annual mutual fund survey or *Money* magazine to determine which mutual funds are available.

When you compare the performance of a fund, look for a good track record over a three-, five-, and ten-year period.

What Type of Fund for You?

Mutual fund objectives fall into several groups. Some growth funds seek capital gains rather than income. Their main objective is to increase the value of the shares by investing in common stocks. Income funds, on the other hand, seek income for their shareholders by investing mostly in bonds. Balanced funds try to get the best of both worlds. They split their assets between stocks and bonds.

Money market funds have also become popular with investors. They enable you to invest money for short periods of time with no penalty for early withdrawal.

Should You Pay a Sales Charge?

Mutual funds are usually operated by management companies and sold through fund distributors. The fund is sold by a direct sales force, through the mail, or by a stockbroker. As I previously stated, there are two main types—no-load and load funds.

A load fund charges the buyer a sales commission based on the amount of the purchase. The commission may run as high as 8 percent or more. Load funds are sold through salespeople, such as stockbrokers.

A no-load fund charges no sales commission but may charge a small withdrawal fee. No-load funds are sold through advertising. (Note: All mutual funds charge a management fee that can range from .20 percent to 2 percent of the assests they manage.)

As an example of the difference between the two types of mutual funds, a $1,000 investment buys $1,000 worth of no-load fund shares but only $915 worth of shares in a fund with an 8.5 percent load.

Do load funds outperform no-load funds? Not necessarily. In the past, there has been no direct correlation between the load paid and the performance of the fund. So always consider a no-load fund when you invest in mutual funds. Just remember that since no-load funds have no sales force, you will have to do your own research to select the one that is right for you.

HOW TO INVEST

If you put $100 a month into a savings account earning 5.5 percent, after twenty years you would have put aside $24,000, and your account would be worth more than $43,000. Not bad. But if you put that same $100 per month into something that earned 12.5 percent (about what a conservative growth mutual fund earns long-term), your account would be worth $107,000.

With these kinds of yields, no wonder investing looks like more fun than saving. But the bigger the potential reward, the greater the risk of losing instead of making money.

Before jumping into investing, you need to know how to invest. These two rules may help: never invest in something you don't understand, and always figure out precisely under what conditions you will sell an investment.

The Pyramid

To take the plunge and start investing, you need to be aware of how to stay afloat. One technique that investors use is called the pyramid of risk approach.

The pyramid model is built on the idea that your investment portfolio should have the right balance of safe, income, and growth investments. At the foundation of the pyramid are safe, secure investments. As you move up the pyramid, the level of risk increases. By using this method, you divide your portfolio according to your investment profile.

If you're young and just starting to invest, you might put 70 percent or more of your assets in growth investments, such as stocks, and split the rest among investments whose objectives are income and safety.

Safe Investments

The safe portion of your investment portfolio provides the basis for your financial strength. Your main objective here is preservation of capital.

Investments in this category include certificates of deposit, available at your local bank or savings and loan. They are issued with maturities of three months to five years or longer. They usually pay interest on a monthly or quarterly basis with a stiff penalty if you cash them in before maturity.

Other safe investments include Treasury bills, notes, and bonds.

Income Investments

Many conservative investors want more than just safety from their investments; they also want high current income. The investor may be a retiree living on a pension and needing additional income or someone in a high tax bracket who wants to keep more of earnings. Whatever the case, the goal is to maximize the current income.

Although the income category includes some safe investments, it also provides a higher return. Two products in the income category are municipal and corporate bonds.

Municipal bonds, issued by counties, cities, and states, are federally tax-free. If you buy these bonds within the state where you live, they may also be exempt from state and local taxes.

Corporate bonds can give you good returns if taxes are not a major concern.

Growth Investments

Increasing your wealth through the growth of your investment dollars should be one of your top priorities. Too many investors have confused investing with speculating, which is just plain gambling. Careful planning and selection can help you minimize risk as you achieve your financial goals.

Investing for growth means accepting a low current yield in return for watching your investment grow in value over the years. Common stocks and real estate are excellent investments for growth.

Other investors have chosen to invest in stocks and real estate through mutual funds. Stock funds have averaged 12 percent a year over the last fifteen years. That means your money would double about every five to six years.

HIGH-YIELD INVESTMENTS

The year 1987 was supposed to be a bonanza for investors looking for income investments. With tax reform, the maximum tax rate dropped from 50 percent to 33 percent in 1987, allowing investors to keep more of the income they earned.

The outlook for fixed-income investments seemed bright; yields on the thirty-year Treasury bond dropped from near 14.0 percent in 1984 to 7.5 percent. Bondholders enjoyed sizable capital gains and income that stayed well above the inflation rate.

Investors were shocked in March and April of 1987 as interest rates started to head upward while bond prices dropped. Bondholders and shareholders in fixed-income mutual funds lost as much as 10 percent of their principal. Still, that has not dampened the appeal of high-yield investments. They include income-producing products that offer above-average returns, higher than money market funds and CDs.

Investors continue to scramble for products such as municipal bonds, mortgage-backed securities, and junk bonds.

High-Yield Bonds: One Way to Earn Above-Average Returns

High-yield bonds, or junk bonds as they are better known, are debt obligations of troubled companies and bonds issued to finance takeovers and other corporate reorganizations. These so-called junk bonds pay as much as 2 to 4 percent more than blue-chip bonds. Junk bonds represent low-rated, often unsecured debt. The 2 to 4 percent higher yield differential is supposed to compensate investors for the additional risk.

As with all bonds, the risks are twofold. The first is market risk. When interest rates go up, all bonds eventually decline in price. The second is credit risk. Will you get your money back? Since World War II, the average default rate for all corporate bonds has been around 1 percent. For low-grade bonds, the default rate has been about 1.5 percent.

The best and safest way to invest in junk bonds is through a high-yield bond mutual fund. In a mutual fund, the portfolio is diversified with twenty or more industries. If one company should default, the effect on the portfolio won't be disastrous.

Choosing a High-Yield Bond Fund

In most successful high-yield bond funds, one issue is not more than 2 percent of the total portfolio. Select a fund that can invest in safer investments, such as government securities, when the market changes.

Look for a family of mutual funds that has a good research department because investing in junk bonds requires research similar to that involved when investing in stocks.

Also, check the average maturity of the bonds in the portfolio. The longer the term of the bond, the greater its exposure to risk. Bonds with maturities of seven to ten years will not fluctuate as much as bonds with twenty- to thirty-year maturities. Carefully read the prospectus and all the sales literature.

High Income with Municipal Bonds

Historically the interest on bonds issued by state and local governments and certain related institutions has been exempt from federal taxes. Income from these bonds is usually exempt from state and local taxes if you live in the state of the issuer. Analysts recommend sticking with high-quality issues rated A or better.

Bonds typically have a face value of $1,000 and are sold in lots of five. If you don't have $20,000 or more to invest, you would probably be wise to invest in a municipal bond mutual fund. They have generally lower minimums and can pay as high as 8 percent, and in addition, they are exempt from federal taxes. For someone in the 28 percent tax bracket, that would be equivalent to a taxable bond paying 11 percent.

INVESTMENT CLUBS

Thinking about investing but don't have a lot of money? An investment club will give you diversification and an educational experience. The clubs work like a mutual fund, with one distinction. You and your fellow investors call the shots.

In an investment club, members pool their money and pick investments as a team. The average club has fifteen members, and each member puts in about $30 per month, according to the National Association of Investors Corporation (NAIC). The NAIC is a national nonprofit organization that currently has more than 100,000 members. It helps member clubs organize and invest, and it maintains that the average club earns 20 percent on its portfolio.

Why Start an Investment Club?

There are several benefits to starting an investment club. If you can get fifteen to twenty people working together in a club, you have funds available to diversify to a much greater extent than any member could on an individual basis.

Sharing research is another advantage. With each member spending an hour or two per week researching investments, a lot of analysis can be produced. Each member gains from the overall research efforts of the group.

Involvement is critical to the success of the club. If two or three people end up doing all the work, a club is not likely to last long. Sharing the duties improves the benefits and profits for everyone in the club. The experience that members gain aids in managing personal investments while adding profits to the club's portfolio.

Organizing Your Club

Every month, about one hundred new investment clubs form and join NAIC. After eighteen months, nearly half of the new clubs are still operating. Setting up an investment club is not difficult as long as you follow simple guidelines.

First, select members from people with whom you have something in common. Schedule a meeting and ask friends and associates to invite their friends. Expect 40 percent to either decline joining or lose interest after several months.

Consider the personalities of the potential members. You should enjoy each other's company. If all goes well, you will be meeting as a group every month and investing together for many years.

Setting Investment Goals

When you're setting up an investment club, determine how much each member will contribute every month. The amount can vary from as little as $10 to $100 or more.

A newly formed club should start out with each member contributing the same amount each month. This standard simplifies record keeping and reporting. Members should see their investments as a long-term venture and shouldn't expect to realize any profits for the first two or three years.

Next, the members should document the club's investment goals in writing.

Final Guidelines

Most investment clubs organize as partnerships with annual profits assigned to members on a per-share basis. This approach is the most manageable one for a club.

You have to anticipate that some people may want to give up their membership. To pay off departing members without disrupting the club's portfolio, invest a portion of the total portfolio in a liquid account—for example, a money market fund.

One of the most crucial guidelines to follow when organizing an investment club is the assignment of responsibilities. It would be wise to include a bookkeeper as a member to assure that accurate records are kept. Every member should spend equal time researching investments and taking care of other club business.

For more information, write the National Association of Investors Corporation, 1515 East Eleven Mile Road, Royal Oak, MI 48067; call 248-583-6242; or check out their Web site at http://www.better-investing.org.

INVESTMENT GIFT IDEAS
FOR CHILDREN

Whenever the holiday season approaches, your thoughts probably turn to gift ideas for your children, grandchildren, nieces, nephews, brothers, and/or sisters. Along with the latest toys, dolls, and games, another gift option you should consider is a financial investment.

Financial products, just like toys or clothing, come in all shapes and sizes. With a little bit of shopping around, you can find one that matches your budget and meets the needs of the recipient—whether the gift be college tuition in fifteen years or money for summer camp in three years.

An investment gift can bring both pleasure and comfort to the giver. The specter of college tuition, for example, strikes fear in the hearts of many parents. The cost of a four-year college education can run as high as $60,000 or more. So, for children born this year, the cost may reach well into six figures at some schools.

Although a forecast like that can put a damper on holiday spirits, there is a bright side. Through careful planning, you can begin to offset these expenses today. By giving relatively small amounts to children while they are young, you can put away enough to take the sting out of the college years looming ahead.

The key is giving money to children early and using appropriate investment vehicles. During their growing-up years, the dividends and interest from their investments will compound at their low tax rate or will be completely tax-free. However, to qualify for the tax advantage, the money must ultimately be used for acceptable purposes such as school tuition, ballet lessons, or summer camp, and not for the child's everyday living expenses. Check your state's laws to find out exactly how this money may be used. Each child may receive as much as

$10,000 per year from an individual, or $20,000 from a couple, without having to pay federal gift tax. A tax-free investment of just $4,000 at 10 percent interest today will blossom into more than $16,500 at the end of fifteen years.

How Should You Give Money to Children?

Building a financial nest egg for children can be easily done by establishing a custodial account, or a trust, under the Uniform Gifts to Minors Act (UGMA). You can work with an investment professional to open this account. You will need a Social Security number for the child and someone to serve as legal custodian for the account. If you are the custodian, the value of the account could be considered part of your estate for tax purposes in the event of your death.

When you set up a trust for a child under the UGMA, the principal and earnings are given to the child permanently. So, be sure you are willing to make a gift that you cannot reclaim at some point later. The IRS carefully scrutinizes UGMA accounts that exceed $30,000. Tax laws change, so consult your tax or legal adviser before you proceed.

You can use a variety of investment products to fund a child's account, for example, zero coupon bonds.

Zero Coupon Bonds

Zero coupon bonds provide a good method for funding a college education. You can purchase these bonds today at a fraction of the value they will have at their maturity. For example, if you purchase $10,000 in zero coupon bonds that are due to mature in ten years, you might pay only about $3,000 for them.

By allowing you to select an issue that will mature at a date when you will need the money, these bonds offer a convenient way to plan for future expenses such as college tuition. These bonds do not pay yearly interest; rather, they pay interest when they mature. However, the interest may be taxable at the child's rate as it accrues every year. One option among zero coupon bonds is the municipal tax-free bond, which is exempt from federal tax.

Mutual Funds

Mutual fund shares as a gift offer several advantages: professional management by experts, safety through a diverse portfolio, and liquidity (easy access to the money).

Not all mutual funds are alike. They offer varying degrees of risk and potential for appreciation. Your investment representative can help you choose a fund that best suits your individual needs. Most mutual fund investment companies have a family of funds; you can switch from one kind of fund to another as your investment goals change.

Aggressive growth funds are at the high-risk end of the mutual fund spectrum. Emerging growth stocks offer shareholders good potential for capital gains. For building college money, an aggressive growth fund would probably provide the best return over the years. These funds are designed to generate high long-term earnings and have, in many cases, performed better than the stock market in recent years. The minimum investment required by these funds is usually $1,000.

Money market funds provide a more conservative option, offering high current income while preserving capital. Money market funds invest in short-term debt instruments, and their value goes up as stocks go down. That is a good reason to have the option of shifting your money within a family of funds as the market changes. Money market funds usually require a $1,000 minimum investment. However, they do not require any fees, and shares can be redeemed at any time.

Stocks

One way to get youngsters' attention is to purchase an investment gift that will have significance. Buying stock in a company such as Walt Disney or Toys R Us that makes a popular toy they like or manufactures clothing they wear can be fun. And the gift need not be expensive. You can purchase a couple of shares of stock in a company, and then if the company has a dividend reinvestment plan, you can have the stock dividends automatically reinvested in additional shares. Some companies will also accept additional cash payments from a shareholder to purchase more stock, usually without brokerage fees.

If the recipients of your investment gift are old enough to follow daily market activity in the newspaper, you can provide them with a unique educational experience as well as a sound investment.

INFLATION

Inflation! There are several types, and some may even help your investment program. The U.S. Department of Commerce has reported that the average annual rate of inflation in the United States, as measured by the consumer price index, was about 3 percent between 1950 and 1970.

Between 1970 and 1980, the average annual inflation rate was 7.8 percent. During the late 1970s, the appearance of 9 to 12 percent rates of inflation worried many investors. In the 1980s, inflation was as high as 14 percent and as low as 2 percent. Over the last several years, inflation has stayed around 3 percent.

Inflation is the economic condition that occurs when the supply of money is out of balance with the supply of things to buy with it. In other words, inflation is too much money chasing too few goods.

That imbalance leads to a sustained increase in prices. Although inflation is not desirable, it can usually be managed. With inflation, you experience an increase in living costs, which puts a squeeze on your budget.

There are at least three types of inflation—cost-push, demand-pull, and printing-press inflation.

Types of Inflation

Cost-push inflation results when an economic force increases the cost of producing goods and services during a specified period, which "pushes up" prices. The force may be external, such as an oil embargo, or production-generated, as with a manufacturer whose production costs increase.

Demand-pull inflation is just the opposite. The demand for goods and services exceeds the available supply. The increased demand "pulls up" prices, resulting in inflation. An example would be the growing number of affluent two-career couples who are searching for housing. This demand may drive up the cost of suburban housing in an area.

Many economists argue that the distinction between cost-push and demand-pull inflation is unimportant. Neither can create a sustained increase in prices unless the Federal Reserve provides an ever-increasing supply of money to accommodate inflation. The Federal Reserve can print more money, creating what is called *printing-press inflation*. With more money chasing a dwindling supply of goods, prices start to rise, and the inflation rate increases.

Printing-press inflation is one of three ways that the government can raise income. The other two ways are imposing taxes and borrowing. Raising taxes is politically unpopular and is used as a last resort. The government can ask people to lend it money by issuing bonds. The U.S. Treasury will sell government debt in the form of Treasury bills, notes, and bonds to investors. The result of this action is anti-inflationary.

Inflation and the Consumer Price Index

Can the consumer price index accurately predict your personal rate of inflation? Inflation is a result of an increase in prices, which is calculated by an index that serves as a representation of the rate of inflation.

The most common index used is the consumer price index. When this index rises or falls, it means that the goods or services measured in the index increased or decreased.

Statements about the consumer price index may be meaningless, however, as they apply to your personal situation. If the index includes the price of a steak and a new house, the index accurately reflects your rate of inflation if you eat meat and buy a new house every month. If you don't buy these items every month, the index does not accurately represent your personal rate of inflation. Your lifestyle gives you a personal inflation rate that may be more or less than the consumer price index.

Misconceptions About Inflation

The rate of inflation affects all of us, but there are many misconceptions about inflation. You have no doubt heard statements like this one: "At the present rate of inflation, a loaf of bread will cost $10 by the time you retire." Several things are wrong with this statement.

First, there has never been a constant rate of inflation in the United States. At times, the rate of inflation has been as high as 14 percent and as low as 1 percent.

Second, salary increases are often tied to an inflation index, which at least helps your salary keep pace with inflation. The next time someone tells you a loaf of bread will cost $10 at a certain date under a given rate of inflation, apply the same growth rate to your salary.

Third, you don't have to buy a loaf of bread at any price. You're free to substitute one item for another, and this substitution can reduce your exposure to inflation.

— 6 —

RETIREMENT

Does God want us to retire?

We tend to see financial planning issues through cultural eyes rather than biblical ones. It is very difficult to find much about the concept of retirement in the Bible. A reference in the book of Numbers indicates that the Levites were to retire from the Tent of Meeting: "This applies to the Levites: Men twenty-five years old or more shall come to take part in the work at the Tent of Meeting, but at the age of fifty, they must retire from their regular service and work no longer" (8:24–25 NIV).

The Levites did not own land or accumulate riches but received their living from the tithes and offerings from God's people. As a reward for their service they were retired at fifty years of age. But if you read into verse 26, you'll see that they could assist their fellow Levites at the Tent of Meeting. So it wasn't a total retirement: "They may assist their brothers in performing their duties at the Tent of Meeting, but they themselves must not do the work. This, then, is how you are to assign the responsibilities of the Levites" (Num. 8:26 NIV).

It appears that instead of retirement, God's people were directed to take sabbaticals. Of course, the first sabbatical was given as a day of rest called the Sabbath: "Six days do your work, but on the seventh day do not work, so that your ox and your donkey may rest and the slave born in your household, and the alien as well, may be refreshed" (Ex. 23:12 NIV). An additional sabbatical was deemed necessary every seventh year: "Six years you shall sow your field, and six years you shall prune your vineyard, and gather its fruit; but in the seventh year there shall be a sabbath of solemn rest for the land, a sabbath to the LORD. You shall neither sow your field nor prune your vine-yard" (Lev. 25:3–4 NKJV).

Studies have shown that when a man retires at age sixty-five, his chances of a fatal heart attack immediately double. Perhaps that is because our minds and bodies were not made for an arbitrary day of shutdown. We should derive pleasure from our work:

> **Then I realized that it is good and proper for a man to eat and drink, and to find satisfaction in his toilsome labor under the sun during the few days of life God has given him—for this is his lot. Moreover, when God gives any man wealth and possessions, and enables him to enjoy them, to accept his lot and be happy in his work—this is a gift of God. He seldom reflects on the days of his life, because God keeps him occupied with gladness of heart.** (Eccl. 5:18–20 NIV)

Doing volunteer work without pay is perfectly legitimate. I am sure your pastor could find many things for you to do around the church and be involved in ministry if you didn't have to worry about getting paid. But as long as you are on this earth, God has work for you to do. The pay may be low or nonexistent. The hours may be short and the work different from what you did in your earlier years, but God has a purpose for your life. God has no desire to take a productive mind and body and per-manently lay them on a tropical island, lose them on a golf course, or park them in a living room watching soap operas, talk shows, and game shows.

I believe it is God's will for us to accumulate sufficient funds, not so that we may retire but so that we may be finan-cially independent and be free to do ministry. In a nutshell, that's all retirement planning is: helping you achieve financial independence. Just think of the work you could do for the Lord, knowing that your and your family's needs will be taken care of. As a financially self-supported Christian involved in ministry, you could have your most fruitful years of ministry ahead of you.

Retirement can be a time of uncertainty. The average couple retire with the home paid for but very little money in the bank. A financial plan can ease the stress.

Your retirement years are a period of major adjustment, both personally and financially. From this point on, you will be living on a fixed income. Although you may have planned during your working years, you will find that inflation requires the use of more income than expected to meet your expenses.

To protect yourself, think about these ideas:

- Consider a part-time job if supplementing your income becomes a necessity.
- Avoid unnecessary spending by budgeting to live on your income.
- Review your insurance again, especially your health coverage. Make sure it is adequate.
- Try to eliminate all debt. A retirement budget should be free from all interest expense and other unnecessary monthly payments.

RETIREMENT PLANNING

Too many investors approach their retirement program as if it were totally separate from their general investment strategy. Nothing could be farther from the truth. (For a quick retirement planner, see fig. 9.)

Your retirement program should be totally compatible with your investment goals. Retirement planning is simply a long-term investment strategy. Your other goals may vary in term from long to short, depending on your objectives.

One of the first things to do when estimating how much you will need for retirement is to make sure you will be able to maintain your present standard of living. To retire financially independent, you will need approximately 65 percent of your present income. By the time you retire, your mortgage will be paid for, your kids will have finished college, and you probably will not have any long-term debt. Therefore, you will be able to live a simpler life.

You should contact the Social Security Administration at 800-772-1213 and ask for a Request for Earnings and Benefits Estimate Statement. You will receive a form similar to the one in figure 12. Upon completing it and mailing it back to the Social Security Administration, you will receive a printout that will detail how much you can expect to receive from Social Security. In addition, there will be a column indicating how much Social Security taxes have been taken out during your working years. Compare this figure with your records to make sure that they match. You should do this at least once every two to three years. And if you have never done it and you are close to retirement, you should do it immediately. The worst time to find out there has been a mistake is when you are one month away from retirement. It could take several months or years to fix the mistake.

Next, several factors will affect how much you will be able to accumulate for retirement. They are inflation, annual contribution (how much you can afford to stash away for retirement), time (how many years before retirement), and yield (what return your money will earn).

Let's use an example:

> Annual income = $30,000
> Years to retirement = 30 (current age = 35)
> Inflation rate = 6%

As I mentioned before, you will need approximately 65 percent of your current income. So, first we multiply $30,000 by .65:

> $30,000
> x   .65
> $19,500

Next, we need to determine how much $19,500 is equivalent to in thirty years, adjusted for inflation. To do this, we use the chart in figure 10 to find your inflation multiplier. Look down the "Years to Go" column, and find your years to go until retirement. Then look across to the column for the inflation rate you wish to assume. Let's assume a 6 percent inflation rate. You now have your inflation multiplier: 5.743.

$$\begin{array}{r} \$19,500 \\ \times\ \underline{5.743} \\ \$111,988.50 \end{array}$$

(We'll round it off to $112,000.)

If you now make $30,000 a year, to retire in thirty years you will need $112,000 in annual income just to maintain your current standard of living. The retirement planning challenge is to have a lump-sum amount of money at retirement that, when invested, would generate $112,000 in income a year.

Let's project a rate of return at retirement of 10 percent. You would need to accumulate a lump sum by age sixty-five that would produce $112,000 in income a year at 10 percent interest. To determine the lump sum needed, we divide the annual income required by the projected rate of return (expressed as a decimal).

$$\begin{array}{r} \$112,000 \\ \div\ \underline{\quad.10} \\ \$1,120,000 \end{array}$$

So the lump sum you need at retirement is $1,120,000.

The retirement planning challenge means that you must match what you know you will need at retirement and how much you must set aside now to accomplish that (see fig. 11). Obviously the higher the rate of return, the more you will have at retirement. To get better returns, you will have to invest in more aggressive investments other than savings accounts and government securities. (For an overview of some of your investment alternatives, see the section in this chapter on investing.)

You need to be concerned about two general classes of retirement programs. The first is a pension plan provided by a corporation, union, or other institution. The second is an individual program, such as an IRA, a Keogh plan, or a Simplified Employee Pension (SEP) plan.

Defined Contribution Plans

Defined contribution plans are structured so that the employer pays a specific amount into the pension fund for each participant. These payments accumulate, along with investment and interest earnings, in separate participant accounts.

Employer contributions may be a percentage of salary or profits. Some of these plans also provide for employee contributions that may be voluntary or mandatory. Your retirement benefits under such a plan will be determined directly by the amount in your account when you retire. As a result, the exact amount of your retirement benefit cannot be known in advance.

The two primary types of defined contribution plans are 401(k) plans and profit sharing.

Defined Benefit Plans

A defined benefit plan is set up so that the amount you will receive at retirement can be determined in advance. Your employer uses a formula to calculate what your benefit will be when you reach retirement age, usually sixty-five.

The formula is one of three general types: a flat-dollar, a career average, or a final-pay formula. Career average and final-pay formulas are most often seen in plans covering nonunion employees. Under pay-related formulas, an employer has some discretion in defining pay for plan purposes. The employer may choose to recognize all compensation, just your base pay, or something in between.

FINANCIAL PLANNING FOR OLDER PEOPLE

Taking good financial care of older people requires advance planning. Here are some tips. Make sure they are getting benefits they are entitled to. Check that registrations for Medicare, Social Security, and other programs are in order. If they are over sixty-five, make sure an additional exemption is taken on federal income taxes.

Older home owners may be eligible for breaks on city and state income and property taxes. Check with the local tax assessor's office. And people over fifty-five who sell their homes are eligible for a one-time capital gains exclusion of up to $125,000. Also check with your local chapter of the American Association of Retired Persons for other programs and information.

Important papers—passbooks, checking accounts, stock certificates, loan papers, and Social Security and Medicare information—should be easily located. Make sure older adults have an updated will. It may even be wise to have a living will, which specifies what kind of care they want to receive if they become very ill. (You or another person should have a copy of the living will. That way, you'll have access to it in an emergency. The original should be stored in a safe place such as a safe-deposit box.)

By helping older relatives arrange their financial affairs now, you can help them avoid costly legal and financial complications later.

Individual Retirement Accounts

Individual retirement accounts, better known as IRAs, have been described as the tax shelter for everyone. The main attraction of the IRA is the tax shelter it provides for your money.

You can gain three tax advantages. First, you may be able to deduct from your income the full amount of your IRA contributions each year. Second, your money accumulates tax-free in an IRA. Any income and capital gains generated by your IRA investment are not taxed until you withdraw the money. And third, by the time you begin withdrawing your IRA money at retirement, your tax bracket should be lower than it was when you earned the money.

Where to Invest Your IRA

Many financial institutions, including banks, brokerage firms, credit unions, insurance companies, and mutual funds, want to offer you their IRAs. Through these institutions, you may place a wide variety of investments in your IRA, including stocks, bonds, mutual funds, limited partnerships, annuities, and certificates of deposit. You may not, however, have precious metals or collectibles in your account.

Depending on how close you are to retirement, you should diversify your investments to provide the right proportion of growth, income, and safety. In the early years, you can focus your objectives on growth. Later, you may want to shift funds into investments that offer a greater degree of safety.

Knowing more about retirement plans will help you prepare for a profitable and comfortable retirement.

SOCIAL SECURITY EXPLAINED

Are you suffering from social insecurity? Smart financial planning demands that you understand what benefits you should expect under Social Security. Three separate funds pay benefits under the Social Security system. The Old Age and Survivors' Insurance Trust Fund provides monthly checks to retirees, their families, and the families of deceased workers. The Disability Insurance Trust Fund pays benefits to disabled workers and their families. The Hospital Insurance Trust Fund pays Medicare claims.

Nearly everyone with earned income must pay Social Security taxes, which will someday pay you benefits. The only persons exempt are some employees of federal, state, and local governments, members of the clergy who decide not to participate, and some employees of foreign companies who work outside the United States.

How to Qualify for Social Security Retirement

To qualify for retirement benefits under the Social Security system, you must have worked long enough and earned enough income to have accrued a specified number of quarters of Social Security coverage. Anyone fifty-nine or younger this year must have accumulated forty quarters to be eligible for benefits. That takes about ten years.

Social Security will add a quarter of coverage to your record every time your earnings reach a specified minimum level. That level rises with inflation. Currently that amount is $500. For every $500 you earn, you accrue one quarter of coverage.

However, each year, you can get credit for a maximum of four quarters of coverage toward your retirement benefits.

What Happens Should You Die Unexpectedly?

Too many people think Social Security benefits only older people. However, in the event of your untimely death, there are Social Security benefits to take care of your loved ones.

Let's say you are a thirty-five-year-old man with a wife and a child. If you have accumulated at least a year and a half of earnings, your spouse and child will be eligible for survivors' benefits. Your child will receive 75 percent of your retirement benefits until age eighteen. This amount can be as much as $9,600 per year. Your wife will also get 75 percent of your benefits as long as she is caring for a child under sixteen; she can receive your full benefit when she reaches sixty-five.

In addition, your family is entitled to $250 for your funeral expenses from Social Security, regardless of your age.

— 7 —

INSURANCE AND INHERITANCE

A LOOK AT INSURANCE

Insurance is a guarantee of repayment after a loss. By purchasing an insurance contract or policy at a comparatively small rate, the purchaser is assured of recovering from a large loss, should it occur. Both possessions and people can be insured. Possessions most often insured include a house and car and personal property. Buildings, boats, collections, businesses, and even an athlete's leg or arm can be insured. The common forms of insurance on people are medical, disability, and life insurance.

Insurance is not specifically defined in Scripture; however, the principle of *restitution,* which means "to restore," is addressed. To restore means to pay someone back for a wrong you have caused. In the area related to finances and insurance, this term usually refers to replacing a material possession and protecting against economic loss. In the books of Exodus, Leviticus, and Deuteronomy, many verses touch on subjects as diverse as payment for theft and responsibility for borrowed goods.

Here are some sample verses from Exodus that would relate to property/casualty or liability insurance:

If men quarrel and one hits the other with a stone or with his fist and he does not die but is confined to bed, the one who struck the blow will not be held responsible if the other gets up and walks around outside with

his staff; however, he must pay the injured man for the loss of his time and see that he is completely healed (Ex. 21:18–19 NIV)

If a man uncovers a pit or digs one and fails to cover it and an ox or a donkey falls into it, the owner of the pit must pay for the loss; he must pay its owner, and the dead animal will be his. (Ex. 21:33–34 NIV)

If a man grazes his livestock in a field or vineyard and lets them stray and they graze in another man's field, he must make restitution from the best of his own field or vineyard. If a fire breaks out and spreads into thorn-bushes so that it burns shocks of grain or standing grain or the whole field, the one who started the fire must make restitution. If a man gives his neighbor sil-ver or goods for safekeeping and they are stolen from the neighbor's house, the thief, if he is caught, must pay back double. But if the thief is not found, the owner of the house must appear before the judges to determine whether he has laid his hands on the other man's prop-erty. In all cases of illegal possession of an ox, a donkey, a sheep, a garment, or any other lost property about which somebody says, "This is mine," both parties are to bring their cases before the judges. The one whom the judges declare guilty must pay back double to his neighbor. (Ex. 22:5–9 NIV)

If a man's bull injures the bull of another and it dies, they are to sell the live one and divide both the money and the dead animal equally. (Ex. 21:35 NIV)

The question that begs to be asked is, Is insurance scrip-tural? Yes, I believe it is. Since God controls everything, we must believe that he has seen fit to let insurance companies be formed that would allow his people to be able to make restitu-tion to individuals who have suffered a loss. But I also think that relying on insurance may have some disadvantages or dangers to the followers of Jesus Christ, who may feel a less urgent need to trust in God. The Bible tells us that God often desires to develop our character through trials and tribulations: "Not only that, but we also glory in tribulations, knowing that tribulation produces perseverance" (Rom. 5:3 NKJV); and "Consider it pure joy, my brothers, whenever you face trials of many kinds, because you know that the testing of your faith develops perseverance" (James 1:2–3 NIV).

If your house burns down, everything is restored, except the items that have sentimental value. When your car gets damaged, it's repaired like new. Suppose you get sick. The doctor and hospital bills will be paid. And when you die, your family will be taken care of for many years. With insurance coverage for these situations, there is no significant material loss.

There was a time when people had to trust God to help them in situations of desperate need. If people got sick, they and their families had to trust God and the Christian community for support. If a house burned down, neighbors and relatives would rally and sacrificially give of their assets of time and money to help someone rebuild. Of course, today friends and neighbors may come around for a brief time and give words of comfort and limited financial gifts, but soon they return to their own lives, barely affected and minimally involved in what has happened.

In the past if a man was injured and could no longer work, his family, church, neighbors, and community would help him. His "insurance" was his involvement in the community. People cared, shared, and prayed. God worked through those relationships to meet not only material needs but also emotional and spiritual needs. Today the injured man's workmen's compensation insurance or disability insurance steps in to provide support where the community could not or would not come forward.

The ideal situation is to have a community plan like the one described in Acts: "There were no needy persons among them. For from time to time those who owned lands or houses sold them, brought the money from the sales and put it at the apostles' feet, and it was distributed to anyone as he had need" (Acts 4:34–35 NIV). In this plan God expects us to count on one another to provide for one another. My insurance plan depends on my connection to the body of Christ and its support during my times of need. It is a self-insured Christian community, that is, the church takes responsibility to care for its members who are ill or disabled, just as the early church did.

God's Word teaches us provision, not protection. God promises to provide for us even if our houses burn down, or we lose our jobs or get sick. The biblical perspective on insurance must be that all resources belong to God. Therefore, the resources that are in the control of an insurance company are still God's. God can work through anything, but his preferred way is not through an impersonal bureaucracy at an insurance company; his preferred way is through people in personal ways.

Since the church in general is not yet spiritually mature enough to make the community plan work, you should carry several types of insurance: life, health, disability, home owner's, and auto. According to the National Insurance Consumer Organization, roughly 10 percent of close to $200 billion spent for insurance is wasted on unnecessary insurance. Often the coverage is redundant or too narrow to be beneficial. A lot of these policies are sold on emotion. In addition, buyers are too befuddled by a myriad of insurance options to know better. The following is a list of types of insurance that you don't need:

- Air travel
- Life, if you are single
- Life on your children
- Cancer
- Rental car, if you have an alternative
- Mortgage
- Credit life
- Health on your pet
- Health that pays $100 a day while you are in the hospital in lieu of comprehensive coverage

LIFE INSURANCE

My experience has been that many Christian couples are underinsured in the area of life insurance. In general, if you are married with children, both husband and wife need at least $500,000 worth of life insurance. The problem usually lies not with the wife, but with the husband. Men think that if they leave too much money to their wives, they will squander it. They often say, "I am not going to leave her money so she can marry some other guy and he will get it." Here is what I say to men who think like that: "You mean to tell me that the wife you love so dearly, the wife who has given birth to your children and helped raise them in a God-fearing household, who has been your helpmate all these years, you would rather that she have to marry the first guy who comes along because she can't support herself and your children on her income? I know that's not what you want. That's not what God would want."

God calls us to provide for our families. At your death if your wife takes the life insurance money and sets fire to it, then that is none of your business. That is between her and God. God calls you to provide the resources so that she will be able to take care of herself and your children, and the financial goals that you developed together can still be fulfilled. A wise move would be to give your wife direction now in what to do with the money that will result in sound financial decisions.

The basic role of life insurance at one time was to provide for your dependents in the event of your untimely death. But today, life insurance is being used as a fund for retirement or children's college educational needs, as an investment vehicle, or as a money source for a variety of other purposes.

Yet buying life insurance can be like walking through a minefield. One false step and you can end up a loser.

You can take two steps that will put you on the road to making the best decision possible in the purchase of life insurance. First, you need to understand the basics of life insurance, and second, you need to find a professional agent to help you select the right policy.

Term Life Insurance

Term, or temporary, insurance was designed to provide policy owners with short-term rather than lifelong protection. It is generally used when a young family needs a large amount of life insurance coverage but is not able to afford a cash-value policy. You purchase term insurance for a certain period of time, one to twenty years. At the end of the term, you can renew the policy or allow it to expire. The premiums increase with each renewal because you are getting older.

Term insurance does not build up a cash value, and it is generally not available after age sixty-five. Properly used, term insurance fills a need for low-cost, short-term protection. However, purchasing term insurance to cover your entire lifetime can well be the most expensive type of policy.

Whole-Life Insurance

There are many variations of cash-value life insurance policies. Most provide the same death benefit throughout your life for a set premium payment.

In a cash-value life insurance policy, you will pay the same premium at age sixty-five as you did when you were thirty. The simplest form of cash-value life insurance is whole-life, or permanent-life, insurance.

The policy remains in force throughout your lifetime. It has the advantage of building up a cash value, which you can use later in several ways. When you retire, for example, you can surrender the policy and take the accumulated cash value.

Universal-Life Insurance

With this type of policy, you have a hybrid product. It is a cross between the lower rates of term insurance and the cash buildup of a whole-life policy. You decide how much you want to pay into your policy each year, with certain minimums applying. You can add extra money one month, then skip several months altogether. If you don't pay enough to cover the cost of the coverage, the extra sum will be subtracted from your cash value.

Shopping for Life Insurance

When shopping for life insurance, don't combine insurance with investments. Buy a life insurance policy for the coverage it provides and not for the investment returns. Buy life insurance to provide for your loved ones in the case of your death, and purchase investments to satisfy investment goals and objectives. To purchase the best policy, first determine how much insurance you need (see fig. 13).

It is always wise to inquire about the actual cost of your insurance. A professional agent should be prepared to give you this information.

Cost information will be given in the form of an index, either a net payment cost or a surrender cost index. The *net payment cost index* is based on the amount paid at your death, and it is useful in comparing policies. The *surrender cost index* is based on what you would get if you turned in the policy. This index is used to compare cash values between policies. With both indexes, a policy with a smaller number is generally a better buy than a comparable policy with a larger number. Knowing how to compare policies and how much to pay will result in your gaining more coverage for less money.

Selecting the Right Policy

When the time comes to actually buy life insurance, look for and select a good agent. First, use an agent who is committed to a career in life insurance sales and is not just a part-time worker. Seek an agent with at least four years' experience in life insurance sales.

Second, look for someone who is a Chartered Life Underwriter (CLU) or is working toward becoming one. This designation identifies a person with substantial knowledge in the field of insurance and other related financial areas.

Third, select an agent who is active in the Million Dollar Round Table. That means you are dealing with an agent who has a successful track record.

In determining how much you should pay for life insurance, see figure 14, which illustrates how much you should pay for term insurance. Then review figure 15, which compares yearly premiums for a $100,000 policy for a nonsmoking male.

Also, before choosing a life insurance company, consult *Best's Guide to Life Insurance Companies*. It is available at your library and rates insurance companies on their overall performance.

Term or Whole-Life?

Well, here I go getting into trouble. Many life insurance agents may not like what I am about to say. But once you have determined how much life insurance you need, buy *all* you need. Suppose that you have completed figure 13, and it turns out that you need $650,000 worth of life insurance. Don't get talked into buying less coverage because your agent wants you to purchase whole-life insurance. It has been my experience that most people can afford to purchase the proper amount of life insurance only if they buy term insurance. I suggest that you purchase twenty-year level term, which means that your coverage and premium will stay the same for twenty years. By the end of that period, your need for life insurance will be greatly diminished—at least that is my prayer for you.

HEALTH INSURANCE

Your health insurance can help you keep your finances fit. With the high cost of medical care today, you have to worry about what will happen to your personal finances if you or a family member becomes sick. If you have health insurance, you can be certain that most of the expenses will be paid.

Here are some features of a health insurance plan. A *basic health plan* is defined as "a policy that includes hospital, sur-gical, and physicians' expenses coverage." Most policies also cover major medical costs. This coverage picks up where your basic coverage ends. Most health insurance policies have a deductible, requiring you to pay the first $200 to $500 of med-ical expenses each year. In addition, a coinsurance clause will have you pay a percentage of certain types of charges, such as prescriptions and doctor visits.

Asset or Liability?

If you're covered by a health insurance plan, chances are, your policy includes hospital expense insurance. These benefits pay for your hospital stay. Your policy should cover room and board, nursing care, drugs, lab fees, X rays, and medical sup-plies. Traditional health insurance plans limit hospital expense coverage to a specified period of time, in most cases from 20 to 120 days. Newer plans now limit the total dollar amount they'll cover.

Another feature of health insurance plans is surgical expense insurance. It covers the cost of operations. But beware that some policies don't cover all procedures. These policies generally list what types of operations they cover and how much they will pay. They typically cover what insurance companies call usual, customary, and "reasonable" fees for surgical procedures.

Major Medical

Without major medical coverage, you can be left footing the entire bill for an extended hospital stay or other medical costs. Major medical insurance picks up where basic coverage—hospital, surgical, and physicians' expenses—ends.

Benefits pay for care provided both in and out of the hospital. For example, if your health insurance limits coverage in a hospital to only twenty-one days and you've been in the hospital twenty-five days, the major medical plan takes effect and pays for the extra four days in the hospital. Most major medical plans pay 80 to 100 percent of your medical expenses over a deductible amount.

HMOs

Health maintenance organizations, HMOs for short, are prepaid health care plans that provide all your medical care. The organization either employs or contracts with physicians in every specialty, from internal medicine to psychiatry.

Most HMOs require you to use their doctors and services, except in emergencies. HMOs give you the cost advantage of no deductibles and no coinsurance. With most plans you pay a nominal fee, say $3 or so, per visit and per prescription. Paying a nominal fee is a major advantage for those who can't afford to pay medical expenses out of pocket. But before you sign with an HMO, check the reputation of the doctors it employs. Also ask these questions: Will the HMO cover accidents when I'm out of town? What happens if I need a specialist not retained by the HMO? Answers to these questions will help you avoid financial surprises later.

Do You Have All You Need?

Finding out how much health insurance you need will help you in purchasing the most coverage for the least amount of money. You want to know three things. First, how much is your deductible? Is it an amount you can afford? Second, does your policy include a coinsurance plan that requires you to pay 20 percent of the bills? At what point would paying 20 percent of your medical costs put you in serious financial trouble? And third, make sure your policy has stop-loss provisions (that is, your maximum out-of-pocket medical expense is limited). If this limit is $2,000, for example, you are protected from paying 20 percent of what could be an enormous medical bill. Also, be sure the policy has a $1 million or higher ceiling on benefits paid by the plan over your lifetime.

DISABILITY INCOME INSURANCE

A disability income insurance policy is a contract between you and an insurance company. You pay a periodic premium, and in exchange the insurance company promises that if you cannot work because you are disabled, it will pay you a percentage of your lost income.

Do You Need It?

Although many people own life insurance because they're aware of the risk of dying, most people ignore the risk of disability. Yet disability is a greater risk for young people. Between the ages of twenty-five and fifty-five, you're more than twice as likely to become disabled as you are to die. Think for a moment about the financial impact on your life if you were unable to work. Could you live without your salary for six months, a year—perhaps longer? If not, you need disability income insurance.

What Determines If You Are Disabled?

The policy's definition of disability determines whether or not you are eligible for benefit payments. The policies that provide the broadest coverage define disability as your inability to perform the duties required by your occupation. A brain surgeon with this type of policy would receive benefits if he couldn't perform surgery, for example, even if he could earn a living as a medical school professor. The policies that provide the narrowest coverage define disability as your inability to work in any job at all. Of course, the broader the coverage, the more expensive the policy.

How Much Do You Need?

Insurance companies don't sell disability policies that replace 100 percent of your salary. If they did, they fear you'd have no economic incentive to go back to work! Expect to find coverage available for 60 to 70 percent of your income. Unless you have substantial other sources of income—from an investment portfolio, for example—it makes sense to buy as much coverage as you can afford.

What Special Policy Features Are Available?

CPI cost-of-living adjustments. This option guarantees that after a year of continuous disability, your benefit amount will increase by an amount pegged to the increase in the consumer price index (CPI).

Automatic increase in benefits. This option provides for a specific increase in benefits for a specified period of time, such as 3 percent a year for five years.

Guaranteed insurability. This option allows you to buy additional monthly benefits without having to provide evidence of your continued good health. It's a way of ensuring that your coverage keeps pace with your rising income and financial obligations.

What Affects Your Rates?

Benefit period. A policy that pays lifetime benefits will be more expensive than a policy that provides benefits for a limited period of time, such as to age sixty-five, or for five years.

Amount of benefit. The greater the benefit, the higher your premium will be.

Waiting period. This is the delay between the onset of disability and the first benefit payment. Waiting periods longer than ninety days will reduce your premium costs.

Definition of disability. The more restrictive the definition of disability used in your policy, the lower the cost.

Features. Inflation riders, return of premium provisions, and other options may be nice, but if their cost puts a policy beyond your budget, stick to the basics—the most important thing is to make sure you have a policy you can afford to maintain.

HOME OWNER'S INSURANCE

Although Americans spend more than $80 billion each year for property and liability insurance, many don't know what they are receiving for their money, and most are unaware of the gaps that exist in their coverage in the form of overinsurance and underinsurance.

Home owner's insurance covers real estate property and personal property against loss. In addition, it protects you against personal liability, medical payments, and property damage caused by persons other than you, the insured.

The term *home owner's insurance* is misleading. Standard packages cover almost everything you own, plus credit card losses, medical bills, and even personal liability. For example, if one of your credit cards is stolen, your name forged, and purchases made without your knowledge, your insurance company will typically pay up to $1,000 toward your losses.

Understanding Your Policy

Home owner's insurance is often thought of as a single type of insurance policy. Four different forms are available for home owners, and two other forms are for renters and condominium owners.

Policies are divided into two sections. Section one deals with property protection and covers your home and its contents. The amount of coverage is based on the cost of replacing the entire house. Your personal property is usually covered up to a limit of 50 percent of the cost of your home.

Section two deals with liability protection. It guards you against personal liability, medical payments to others, and damage to other people's property. The range of coverage under a standard policy can be enormous. However, you are covered only for losses named in the policy unless you have all-risk coverage, as in a policy that is type HO-3 (see fig. 16 for explanation).

How Much Insurance Do You Need?

Selecting the right amount of home owner's insurance means looking in the right place. Focus your attention on section one in your policy. Indicate that the house and its contents are to be insured for replacement cost. Then if there is a loss, you are given money to actually replace, repair, or rebuild your house and replace its contents.

To get an idea of the importance of having replacement cost coverage on your personal property, imagine this scenario. Someone breaks into your home and steals your $500 television that you have owned for five years. If you have actual cash-value coverage on your personal property, then your insurance company will first determine that the television has a useful life of, say, ten years. That means that the television loses $50 in value each year ($500 divided by ten years). You have owned the television for five years, so the insurance company will hand you a check for $250 ($50 times five years) to purchase a replacement television that cost you $500. And because of inflation, your $500 television now costs $550. So you will have to come out of your pocket with a total of $300 to replace your television.

If you had replacement cost coverage on your home owner's policy, then your insurance company would give you the money to go out and purchase a television that most closely resembles the one that was stolen, even if it costs more than what you originally paid for it.

Insure your personal property for every dollar value of property you have in your home. If your property is worth $80,000, buy $80,000 worth of insurance for your personal property.

Updating Your Insurance

Review and update your home owner's insurance every year. The value of your home and possessions fluctuates. Some policies have an inflation guard feature that allows the value of your home to keep pace with inflation, but that may not be enough. Reviewing your policy annually will keep your coverage in line with the value of your possessions.

Besides being insured, you must be able to prove what you have. Take a complete inventory, listing and describing every item you own. Note the purchase price and the estimated date you bought it.

If you own video equipment, you can make a personal inventory by videotaping the entire house. Or you can use a camera to take photos. Keep a copy of the tape or photos and list outside your home, perhaps in a safe-deposit box. In the event of fire, they would not be destroyed.

Getting the Best Deal

Prices for home owner's insurance can vary, but there are some ways you can make sure to get the best deal. Above all, shop around. Compare rates on similar policies (see fig. 16). Consider buying all your insurance policies from the same agent or company. You may be able to get a price break if the same insurer writes the coverage on your auto insurance as well.

Many insurers offer discounts up to 10 percent if you install various safety and security features in your home, such as fire and smoke alarms, deadbolt locks, and fire extinguishers. You can also cut your rates by raising the amount of your deductible, the amount you pay before the insurance takes over. Although your home owner's insurance is a necessary part of your insurance coverage, it doesn't have to cost you an arm and a leg.

CAR INSURANCE

Careful shopping will uncover bargains in car insurance (see fig. 17). Car insurance rates continue to climb as inflation is subdued. It pays to periodically review your coverage to see that it's adequate, not excessive or overpriced.

In a recent survey, insurance companies were asked for rates on a policy covering a husband, a wife, and a seventeen-year-old son living in a northeastern city, all with flawless driving records. The highest yearly premium was more than $1,400, while the lowest was almost $600.

The drastic differences were attributed to several factors, including marketing methods and the amount of commissions paid to agents. If you are patient and willing to invest time, you can find a policy that fits your needs and your wallet.

Liability Coverage

Liability protection is a vital part of your car insurance. Making sure you have enough liability coverage can save you from financial disaster. If you injure somebody and are found liable, your liability insurance pays for the victim's medical and hospital expenses, rehabilitation, nursing care, lost income, and "pain and suffering." Your coverage is good only up to the policy limits. You can be held personally responsible for any excess that the insurance does not cover.

Liability coverage is mandatory in most states, and typical coverage is $25,000 per person, $50,000 per accident (bodily injury), and $10,000 for property damage. This is usually stated as 25/50/10.

Insurance experts insist that this coverage is not sufficient. They state that minimums of $100,000 per person, $300,000 per accident, and $50,000 for property damage are more realistic.

Ways to Save Money

If you are willing to take on just $200 worth of risk, you may save money on your collision and comprehensive coverage.

Collision insurance pays for damage to your car if an accident is your fault or if an at-fault driver doesn't have insurance. Comprehensive insurance protects you against fire, theft, vandalism, and other disasters.

The key to saving money on collision and comprehensive is the deductible—how much you are willing to pay before the insurance takes over. Deductibles for this type of coverage generally range between $50 and $500. The higher the deductible, the lower the premium. You may be wise to choose the highest deductible you can afford to pay without seriously disrupting your finances.

Optional Coverages

By eliminating or minimizing certain types of optional coverage, you can save money on car insurance.

If you have high-limit health insurance, you may not want no-fault or medical payments coverage. No-fault coverage is mandatory in many states but optional in others. It pays medical expenses regardless of who is at fault. Medical payments coverage is similar but optional in many states also. No-fault or medical payments coverage could help if your health insurance is not enough.

Discounts

You may qualify for special discounts on your auto insurance. When you're shopping for auto insurance, ask each company to provide a list of the discounts available in addition to the amount you will have to pay for the coverage you want.

Discounts of up to 40 percent are available for good driving. The requirements may vary, but you may qualify if you haven't had any moving violations or chargeable accidents in the last thirty-six months. A course in driver training or defensive driving may lower your premiums. If your car has air bags or automatic safety belts, your premium may be lowered. A few companies have lower premiums for nonsmokers and drivers who don't drink.

If you consolidate your coverage with one company by insuring more than one vehicle, you may be eligible for a discount. Get at least three quotes from several insurance companies as you shop, and check with your current insurance agent before making any changes.

To help you compare auto insurance policies, consider calling Consumer Reports Auto Insurance Price Service (800-807-8050). Be prepared to provide the makes and models of your cars, drivers in your household, driving records, annual mileage, and how much insurance you want. Then, for $12, the service will compare as many as seventy policies and give you a list of up to twenty-five of the lowest-priced policies.

INHERITANCE

One of our highest callings as Christian parents is to leave our children a financial inheritance as well as a godly heritage. We all know that training in knowing the ways of God will be a point of reference to guide them the rest of their lives: "Train a child in the way he should go, / And when he is old he will not depart from it" (Prov. 22:6 NKJV). But God equally demands that we leave them resources upon which to fulfill their ministry in the world:

> *A good man leaves an inheritance for his children's*
> *children,*
> *but a sinner's wealth is stored up for the righteous.*
> (Prov. 13:22 NIV)

> *Houses and wealth are inherited from parents,*
> *but a prudent wife is from the LORD.* (Prov. 19:14
> NIV)

It is an irresponsible act and the poorest sort of stewardship to pass on money and assets to anyone who has demonstrated he or she is incapable of handling it with a view toward eternity. We should entrust money to our children after our death only if we would trust them with it now. Stories abound about children squandering the wealth left to them by their parents who had very good intentions. Given a large sum of money, children can quit work or slack off and become accustomed to having whatever they want and doing whatever they want.

Our duty as Christian parents is to entrust at least a small amount of our estates to our children while we are still alive, as in the parable of the prodigal son: "The younger one said to his father, 'Father, give me my share of the estate.' So he divided his property between them" (Luke 15:12 NIV). Although the prodigal in this story got his entire inheritance and then went out and squandered it, I am suggesting giving our children a partial advance. If we do this, we can offer them guidance about what to do with the money. Once they have demonstrated that they are good stewards, we will feel more comfortable about how much we leave them. Leaving money with no wisdom is not God's way:

> *Wisdom, like an inheritance, is a good thing*
> > *and benefits those who see the sun.*
> *Wisdom is a shelter*
> > *as money is a shelter,*
> *but the advantage of knowledge is this:*
> > *that wisdom preserves the life of its possessor.*
> (Eccl. 7:11–12 NIV)

We will discuss children and money more thoroughly in Chapter 9.

ESTATE PLANNING

Estate planning is the process by which you prearrange your financial matters for the benefit of your family or other beneficiaries after your death. For some, death is difficult to talk about, and estate planning discussions can become quite emotional. However, wise use of available estate planning techniques can be of considerable benefit to you by alleviating the worry of leaving a family in a state of financial hardship.

Estate planning was once regarded as a concern of only the wealthy. That's because at one time, the primary reason for estate planning was to avoid federal estate taxes. Today, most people should have an estate plan, regardless of the size of their estate. No matter how rich or not so rich you are, you have an estate. It consists of all of the assets and liabilities you have at the time of your death.

One myth of estate planning is that it's for older people. Younger people actually risk more by failing to plan. Suppose you and your spouse die at the same time, leaving two young children? If you leave no wills, the state will decide who raises your children.

Organizing Your Affairs

The estate planning process has six steps:

1. Organize your financial affairs.
2. Determine your total estate.
3. Identify problem areas.
4. Formulate the plan.
5. Put the plan into action.
6. Review and revise it on a regular basis.

Organizing your affairs requires that you keep information regarding your financial advisers, bank accounts, employment data, budgets, and balance sheets. In addition, insurance records, investment data, tax returns, wills, deeds, and titles to property should be kept together.

Gather up birth, marriage, and/or divorce papers, and keep them in a safe and central location. If you organize now, you will help your loved ones by making important documents accessible after your death.

Identifying Goals

The hardest part of estate planning is identifying goals. This process will be easier if you have personal financial goals already in place.

Your estate planning goals are designed to ensure that your family's financial goals remain intact. These goals may include funding retirement plans, financing a college education for your children, and providing family support should sudden death occur.

To assure a well-thought-out plan, be realistic, be complete, stay flexible, and include your family in the planning process. It is your life and estate, but your family will have to live with the decisions after you are gone.

The Plan

In estate planning, you may choose from several ways to achieve the same goal. To decide which alternatives are right for you, you need to know something about inflation, insurance, investments, taxes, and much more. Get the advice of an attorney, a financial planner, and specialists in life insurance, taxes, and other areas. Keep this plan up-to-date by revising it periodically.

Your Will

Your will is the cornerstone of your estate plan. If you die without a will, you die intestate. That means the state will decide how your estate is to be distributed. Without a will, even the simplest procedures have to be cleared by the court, costing time and money.

The surest way to avoid problems is to make an attorney part of your estate planning team. Each state has peculiarities in administering or handling wills and estates. Acceptable moves in one state—such as disinheriting a child—could be illegal in another state. Anything illegal presents grounds for challenging your entire will.

A simple will may cost several hundred dollars to draft, but done properly, it assures that your wishes are carried out after you are gone.

About three out of ten Americans die before retirement. Yet seven out of ten die without a will. Many of us don't like to think about death, but we will all die eventually. It is God's will that we provide for our families, and making sure we have made provision in case of death is part of that responsibility. If we really love our families, we'll bite the bullet and give serious thought to writing a will.

Attorneys say if you're single with no assets, a will may not be important. But if you're married or have children, you definitely need a will.

Will Kits

Saving money is a good idea, but not in preparing a properly written will. Since probate law is very complicated, attorneys say too many things can go wrong if you try to write your will yourself. Chances are, you'll leave some things out.

In a will, it's not enough to say who is to get what portion of your property. You must give your executors the power to carry out your wishes in disposing of your property.

Some attorneys are skeptical of will kits, saying too many variables exist in the laws from one state to another. There is no way they can all be covered in a kit.

You can expect an attorney to charge up to $500 to properly prepare a will.

Minor Children

It may seem to be the best way to provide for your children's future, but listing your minor children as beneficiaries on your life insurance policy could cause major problems if you die while they are underage.

In many states, children cannot collect money without a court-appointed guardian. The guardian must be bonded, making the whole procedure expensive and complicated. Attorneys say these problems can be avoided if you make your life insurance payable to your estate. Then in your will, set up a testamentary trust for your children, thereby avoiding the need for guardianship. A will should also stipulate who would have custody of your minor children.

What to Include

A will is a tool to get a job done. That job is to clearly state what happens to your property after you are gone. But you won't be there to explain what you meant, so the will must be clearly written and should include certain stipulations.

Attorneys suggest that a will should name an executor and an alternate. If you have minor children, your will can name a guardian for them. If there is a trust for the children, the will should name a trustee.

A will should dispose of your property and give powers to the executor.

Avoid leaving specific dollar amounts to heirs because they come off the top of the estate and could leave nothing for persons farther down the list.

You shouldn't put funeral and burial instructions in a will since it is usually not read until after the funeral.

Where to Keep Your Will

Writing an up-to-date will is an essential part of being financially responsible. But if no one knows where your will is, it will do your heirs no good.

Lawyers say you should keep a copy of the will at home. But store the original off the premises, perhaps in a safe-deposit box. In most states, wills can be filed in the county courthouse for safekeeping.

Be sure to replace the original if you make any changes in your will. Your marriage or divorce will revoke a previous will. Also, if you inherit any money, you should update your will. As a rule of thumb, review your will every three to five years.

CHOOSING YOUR FINANCIAL ADVISERS

Choosing the right financial advisers will save you time and money. If you're like most people, you don't have the time it takes to properly manage your finances. Trusted financial advisers can provide you with knowledge, research, and wise counsel, thereby reducing the amount of time you must invest. Your financial advisers will also save you money. They will not only help you get the desired return on your investments and assist you in selecting the right strategies, but they will also keep you from making costly mistakes.

A FINANCIAL PLANNER

A lot has been written about financial planning and financial planners. Although no legal definition of the term exists, *financial planning* generally involves evaluating and recommending strategies to help you achieve your financial goals. Planning advice should be objective and comprehensive. It should coordinate your investment purchases with other aspects of your financial life. For instance, you may want advice about employee benefits, college costs, taxes, retirement, and estate planning. The title *financial planner* also not legally defined, is used by a variety of individuals—accountants, brokers, and insurance agents, for example—to imply that they offer comprehensive financial planning services.

Decide If You Need a Financial Planner

Not everyone needs the advice of a financial planner. If you do your homework (such as reading the many publications geared to helping you make the best use of your money or taking objective financial education courses), you can undertake your own financial planning. Even if you decide to hire a financial planner, you still need to know as much as you can about your individual financial situation. Without that knowledge, it's nearly impossible to evaluate whether a planner's recommendations make sense for you.

Although financial planners can help you make investment decisions, in general hiring a planner presumes you have discretionary income to invest. Many experts say you shouldn't consider most investments until you have financed some basic living items, such as housing, insurance, a cash reserve fund for emergencies, and retirement plans available through your employer. If you can't meet these (and other) financial needs, you may decide you need help not in investment planning but in basic money management. The right planner may be able to help you set up a budget and monitor it so that you can move from short-term spending to saving for future goals.

What to Expect from a Good Financial Planner

If you decide to use a financial planner, a good one should assist you in the following ways:

- Assess your relevant financial history, such as tax returns, investments, retirement and estate planning, wills, and insurance policies.
- Review your net worth statement, examine your debts, and determine if any should be consolidated, paid off from other available funds, or refinanced.
- Help you develop a financial plan, based on your per-

sonal and financial goals, history, preferences, and psychological investment risk level.

- Identify areas where you need help, such as building up a retirement income, improving your investment returns, buying or selling an insurance policy, and reducing taxes.
- Write down and discuss an individualized financial plan and work plan (time table) that you both understand and are willing to sign.
- Help you implement your financial plan, including referring you to specialists, such as lawyers or accountants, if necessary.
- Review your situation and financial plan periodically and suggest changes in your program as needed.

Guidelines for Selecting a Good Financial Planner

There are several ways to look for a financial planner. One place to start is to look for planners who are certified. Certification does not guarantee that a person will be a wise or creative planner. It does indicate, however, that he or she has studied important subjects in the financial planning field, such as wills, trusts, investments, taxes, home ownership, and life and health insurance.

The major groups that represent financial planners who have taken courses and passed examinations are: the National Association of Personal Financial Advisers (NAPFA); the Registry of Financial Planning Practitioners of the International Association for Financial Planning (IAFP); the Institute of Certified Financial Planners (ICFP); and the Chartered Financial Consultants (ChFC).

You can get a list of names of those financial planners in your area who are certified by writing to these organizations. (The addresses are at the end of this section.)

Registered Investment Advisers are people who furnish investment advice for a fee and are required to register with the Securities and Exchange Commission. This does not indicate that they are financial planners or have had any special training. By law, however, they are supposed to disclose their educational backgrounds and financial planning experience on a federal government form called Form ADV. The registration form, Form ADV, is divided into two parts.

Part one covers information used by the Securities and Exchange Commission (SEC) to evaluate the adviser's application. It includes detailed information about the applicant's disciplinary history, including civil or criminal actions against the applicant and disciplinary actions by federal and state regulatory agencies and self-regulatory organizations.

Part two of Form ADV includes extensive information that advisers are required to disclose to potential clients, such as the method of compensation, affiliation with other financial industry activities, education, and types of service offered.

Recommendations of friends and colleagues may play a role as you select a financial adviser. But an investment adviser who impresses one client may be unsuitable for someone else. Select a firm or individual who has the skills and expertise to meet your specific needs, including being sensitive to how much risk you are willing to take with your investments.

Beware of planners who use high-pressure tactics or promise unusually high rates of return. Remember, no investment is so good that you can't go home first to think it over. Check with the local Better Business Bureau and Office of Consumer Affairs as well as the professional associations and the Securities and Exchange Commission (SEC) to see if any complaints have been lodged against the planner you are considering. Be aware, however, that because years may pass before investments are found to be worthless, it may take time before complaints surface against a particular financial planner.

Determining Fees

Financial planners are paid in a variety of ways. Ask specifically how the fee is calculated and what it will be. Explore some of the following arrangements to see which fee option serves your interests best:

Fee-Only Financial Planners

Fee-only planners base their charge on gathering your financial data, analyzing it, recommending a plan of action and helping you implement it. They do not earn income from the financial products they might suggest you buy. You may pay some costs to unaffiliated companies for investment and insurance products. Your planner should be able to estimate these costs. Hourly or flat fees are most common. Payment is required whether or not you implement the suggested plan.

Commission-Only Planners

Some planners charge no fee for service to their client but make their money through commissions paid by the marketers of the investment products they sell. For example, if a client buys insurance on the advice of a financial planner, the planner will not charge the client for that advice but will receive a commission from the insurance company. If your planner earns a commission, make sure you get a disclosure of the commission you will pay before recommended investments are implemented. Since commissions are often not disclosed, it is difficult to know how much you are paying your adviser and whether, for example, the fee was necessary at all. (Commissions on mutual funds can average about 5 percent; commissions on insurance can be 50 percent or more of the first year's premium. Generally, higher risk products offer the highest commissions.) Some commission-only planners might be inclined to direct your financial plan toward the purchase of products that provides them with the best commissions. Therefore, until you develop a trusting relationship with a planner who knows your complete financial picture, you may want to exercise caution in following the advice of someone who works solely on commission. As a prerequisite for doing business, make a written agreement to disclose yearly total commissions earned by the planner and the planner's broker/dealer on recommendations made to you.

Fee and Commission Planners

Some financial planners receive payments from both a sales commission and a fee. If the planner receives a commission from the company that sells the product you purchase, the fee you are charged may be less. No matter which fee structure you work with, make sure you get a written estimate of what services you can expect for what price. Compare this estimate with others and select the package of services that best meets your needs at a reasonable cost.

Resources

The International Association for Financial Planning
Registry of Financial Planning Practitioners
Two Concourse Parkway, Suite 800
Atlanta, GA 30328
404-395-1605

The Institute of Certified Financial Planners
Two Denver Highlands
10065 East Harvard Avenue, Suite 320
Denver, CO 80231-5963
1-800-282-7526

Chartered Financial Consultants
The American College
270 Bryn Mawr Avenue
Bryn Mawr, PA 19010
215-526-1000

National Association of Personal Financial Advisers
1130 Lake Cook Road
Suite 150
Buffalo Grove, IL 60089
1-800-366-2732

INSURANCE AGENTS

Your insurance agent is an important player on your team of professional financial advisers. The best agent will sell you the type and amount of coverage you need. You should buy life, health, and disability insurance from a life insurance agent. If you're seeking home owner's or auto and liability coverage, a property and casualty agent is the one to consult. Most agents tend to specialize in only one group of products, so you may want to work with more than one agent.

You may not need an insurance agent at all if you know what type of insurance you want and how much you need. You can buy from some of the low-cost companies that sell by telephone. However, for most people, an insurance agent is necessary. There are two different types of agents: the direct and the independent.

Agents who work for just one company are referred to as *captive agents* or *direct writers*. They can sell insurance offered by only one company. That is fine if the company's products are competitively priced across the board, but often they are not.

Independent agents, on the other hand, work for a number of insurers. They may be able to fit you with the right coverage, or they may promote a company's product because it pays them a larger commission. You should base your decision on the price of the coverage and the agent's competence.

The Right Agent for You

Before you try to select an agent to satisfy your insurance needs, you should understand how much coverage you will need and how much it will cost you.

Get quotes from four or five agents recommended to you by friends and associates. Use these quotes to narrow down your choice of agents to two or three you feel are the most competent. Stick with agents who do most of their business with companies rated A+ in *Best's Insurance Reports,* available at your local library.

Finally, limit your list of choices to agents who have been working full-time at least four years. This work record shows a commitment to the profession. In addition, look for the following professional designations because they indicate added experience and knowledge: CPCU (Chartered Property/Casualty Underwriter) and CLU (Chartered Life Underwriter).

— 8 —

YOUR MARRIAGE AND MONEY

To understand what the Lord said about money, we have to go back to our marriage vows. Not the ones that we made up for the wedding ceremony, but the one that God gave to his people: "For this reason a man will leave his father and mother and be united to his wife, and they will become one flesh" (Gen. 2:24 NIV). If we are to become what God intended, then we need to become like one. I now strive to be my wife's partner in life, and we must share everything, including our money. There is no more mine and hers; it's ours. When God said that two will become one, that means what's hers is mine, and what's mine is hers. We share.

You would be surprised to find out that many spouses don't even know the other's salary. These couples generally don't stay married very long, and if they do stay married, they don't know the intimacy that results from sharing.

Years ago people got married relatively young, around twenty-one years of age. Today many people are getting married at a later age. Adults who marry for the first time may be age thirty or beyond. The result is that when people do finally get together, they may have built up substantial assets: a car, savings, investments, a house, and maybe a business. So there is more to share—at least we would think so. But I have counseled couples with separate bank accounts and cars. Generally they keep all their financial assets separate. They may contribute to a fund for the house expenses or mutual goals, but beyond that, they are free to do with their money whatever they wish. If one person in the marriage makes more money, watch out! It becomes a controlling mechanism. That spouse uses it to bully the other into doing what he or she wants with the family finances. That is not God's way. I believe when God said that two will become one, money must be part of the equation. If you are truly going to know the intimacy that comes from sharing resources, here is how your household should operate.

All the money that comes into the household goes into one checking account, and the bills are paid from that account. Each spouse receives an allowance to take care of any expenses, including lunches and transportation costs (buses, trains, or tolls). Each is free to spend that money as he or she chooses. The allowance should be the same for each spouse, regardless of how much money each brings in. This is how my wife, Barbara, and I function in our household. As matter of fact, we functioned this way before I was saved. So when I started studying God's Word, I came to the understanding that I was practicing a biblical principle. This principle allowed us to save almost her entire paycheck that would go toward building up a reserve that would finance our own business. And you know, it worked! It will work for you, too, if both you and your spouse work.

You have a tremendous opportunity to achieve financial goals that your parents only dreamed about. But remember, money is never going to make you happy. Don't spend your life doing urgent things rather than important things. If you have spent your whole life trying to keep up with the Joneses, you'll discover at age sixty-five that when you finally caught up with them, you still weren't happy. But then that is what this whole book is about.

The handling of money can function as a doorway to intimacy, helping you and your spouse to know each other better. God can use money to illustrate the following biblical truths:

TO DRAW YOU CLOSER

You enter marriage feeling that you and your spouse are the perfect couple. Reality sets in eventually, and you realize that your marriage union is not perfect. As you and your spouse grow closer and become more intimate with each other, the "real you" comes out. Your shortcomings become apparent, and you let your hair down, so to speak. The best marriages are not the result of a perfect union of personalities. No one is perfect, and every marriage requires making adjustments. The best marriages are made by two people who, once they recognize their differences, remain committed to each other for better or for worse. They learn how to work through their differences and become a stronger couple because of that struggle. Money issues can definitely bring out the worst and best in a couple. Nothing brings out your true self like facing financial decisions. Nothing will draw you closer or apart than how you and your spouse relate concerning money.

TO HELP YOU COMMUNICATE AND COOPERATE

It is difficult, if not impossible, to make successful financial decisions as a couple without learning how to get along with each other. Satan doesn't want you to get along. He hopes that by fostering strife and discord, the resulting turmoil will drive you away from God. If you keep God's Word as your financial guide, trusting in him to give you guidance in your financial decision making, then you will indeed be brought closer together through your mutual submission to his wisdom in financial affairs.

Together you have to decide what kind of car you will drive, house you will live in, clothes you will wear, and vacations you will take. You have to consult each other about the types of investments you want to make. Of course, keep in mind that you and your spouse will often approach things from different perspectives. Let me give you an example. In making financial decisions I usually come from a utilitarian perspective; my wife, on the other hand . . . let's just say she is a little more extravagant. Take clothes, for instance, I think that all we need is enough clothes to last a week. In fact, I would wear the same pants for several days. My rationale is that clothes are just to cover the body. We need to buy clothes only once and then make alterations. My wife likes to have a different outfit for every day of the month. (Husbands, you know what I'm talking about.) As a couple, we have come to an agreement about what is acceptable for us as a family when we buy clothes. We still have our differences. I see her point of view and she sees mine, but because we believe that it is the Lord's will for us to develop and maintain a budget, our solution is determined by how much we have allocated in our budget for spending on clothes. The process of discussing it helped us practice how to communicate without being hurtful and to cooperate to come to a solution to our dilemma. In addition, we learned something about each other that strengthens our relationship.

TO DEVELOP FAITHFULNESS

Our response to financial problems is a good indicator of whether we trust God or whether we just *say* we trust God. In other words, when the heat is on, we find out what people are really made of. We find out if they are still willing to be obedient to God and do it his way. Shadrach, Meshach, and Abednego demonstrated that even if they were to be burned up, they would not worship false gods: "If we are thrown into the blazing furnace, the God we serve is able to save us from it, and he will rescue us from your hand, O king. But even if he does not, we want you to know, O king, that we will not serve your gods or worship the image of gold you have set up" (Dan. 3:17–18 NIV).

God bestows wealth on us, no matter how small or great, to test our faithfulness or loyalty. He does this to see how we will handle the good times. Often it is not during the bad times that we have a problem following Jesus. But when things are going well, we tend to think that we caused the success. So how we handle wealth and success gives God a clue to how we would handle true spiritual riches of the kingdom of heaven: "Whoever can be trusted with very little can also be trusted with much, and whoever is dishonest with very little will also be dishonest with much. So if you have not been trustworthy in handling worldly wealth, who will trust you with true riches?

And if you have not been trustworthy with someone else's property, who will give you property of your own?" (Luke 16:10–12 NIV).

TO JUMP-START YOUR PRAYER LIFE

When we are at the end of our financial rope, we often turn to Jesus. If you have never gotten down on your knees and prayed to God that some financial burden be lifted, don't worry. If you live long enough, you will. Financial stress can deepen a prayer life. Take it from me, I know. God can use a financially difficult time in your life to get you to commune with him more often so that you can get to know him better, to learn his ways so that you can find out his will for your life.

I remember when I was building my business, I often didn't know how I was going to make it to the next week. But I continued to pray that God's will be done in my life. I prayed that I would receive that contract so that I could support my family. And you want to know something? I sometimes didn't receive that contract, but I was always able to take care of my family. I knew it had a lot to do with my prayer. My prayer sounded very similar to Jacob's in Genesis 28: "Then Jacob made a vow, saying, 'If God will be with me and will watch over me on this journey I am taking and will give me food to eat and clothes to wear so that I return safely to my father's house, then the LORD will be my God and this stone that I have set up as a pillar will be God's house, and of all that you give me I will give you a tenth'" (Gen. 28:20–22 NIV).

In addition to praying, like Jacob, I stayed obedient to God. I continued to go to church and live a Christian life. I didn't stop tithing. God honors his Word. Never did he leave me or forsake me. I knew that no matter what happened, as long as I continued to do his will, everything would be all right. And it was and still is. (I will discuss more fully your prayer life and money in Chapter 12.)

TO CLARIFY WANTS AND NEEDS
(LIFE VALUES)

You can't have it all. And even if you could, you probably wouldn't be satisfied:

Whoever loves money never has money enough;
  whoever loves wealth is never satisfied with his
    income.
  This too is meaningless.
As goods increase,
  so do those who consume them.
And what benefit are they to the owner
  except to feast his eyes on them? (Eccl. 5:10–11 NIV)

Many worldly temptations will clamor for your attention. Listed among the fruit of the Spirit is self-control: "But the fruit of the Spirit is love, joy, peace, patience, kindness, goodness, faithfulness, gentleness and self-control. Against such things there is no law" (Gal. 5:22–23 NIV). The ability to demonstrate moderation or restraint in your financial affairs will keep you away from money troubles. In the United States, the inability to stop spending is a prescription for trouble: "Like a city whose walls are broken down / is a man who lacks self-control" (Prov. 25:28 NIV).

Since you can't have it all, God can use money to help you and your spouse learn to clarify your life values, determine your financial priorities, and make wise choices. Your ability to do these things will tell a great deal about your spiritual maturity.

And if you allow him to, God can use money to draw you and your spouse closer, assist you in achieving your financial goals, and help you fulfill his will in your lives. Studies have shown that the most powerful economic unit is a married couple. A husband and a wife can achieve more together than they could separately. This one-flesh union will prove to be the most dynamic, interesting, and rewarding part of your life—if you keep God first.

— 9 —

YOUR KIDS AND
MONEY

To find out what kids today know about money, a nation-wide survey was conducted to test the consumer knowledge of high school seniors. The survey was developed by experts in the fields of business, government, and personal finance. The test covered most of the basics young adults have to deal with, such as banking issues involving checking, savings, and credit. Spending areas included shopping for groceries, renting an apartment, and buying and maintaining a car. The teenagers tested were a diverse group representing the ethnic makeup of America and all income levels.

The results from the test yielded no surprises concerning the consumer and personal finance knowledge of our youth. Today's teenagers are financially illiterate and are not prepared to cope with the world as consumers. The teenagers' average score on the entire test was 42 percent.

An examination of the financial lives of adults reveals that their lack of basic money management skills has resulted in poor financial decisions. Bankruptcy rates are skyrocketing, and consumers feel inadequate to plan their financial lives. In recent years financial institutions, primarily banks, have increased their efforts to help adult consumers learn how to do everything from buying a house to investing in mutual funds. In addition, many firms, including MasterCard and VISA, have developed programs to help teens and college students understand how to manage money, especially credit. You would think that with all the emphasis on this subject matter, our educational system would respond with incorporating basic money management curriculum in the schools. Well, it hasn't.

For several years, I wrote a personal finance column for the *Atlanta Constitution/Journal*. In one column I asked readers to respond to this question: Should teenagers have to pass a course on personal finance in order to graduate from high school? A whopping 93 percent said yes! The respondents represented a cross section of the community, including teachers, students, business executives, and parents. The column that I wrote as a result of that survey prompted the Federal Reserve Bank to lead an effort along with other financial institutions from around the country to try to get more personal financial education in the schools.

It is my belief that until it becomes mandatory for students to take personal finance–related classes, we will have financially illiterate children who will grow up to be financially illiterate adults. So for now, the best place for kids to learn about money is at home.

What makes money a taboo subject in many households? Apparently the emotional debates that parents often have about it. But mothers and dads should agree on this: it's important to get an early start teaching the children basic financial concepts that God has laid down in his Word. If we want to help our children avoid the mistakes that many of us have made, then we need to start now.

As a parent, you need to help your children grow in the area of personal finances, but you need to do it in the larger context of teaching them God's Word and principles on how to develop a relationship with God. You must also understand that children do what they see adults do. In other words, children will respond not only to what you say but also to what you do in everyday life. You can tell your children one thing, but if you practice something entirely different, they will pick up on that:

> **But as for you, continue in what you have learned and have become convinced of, because you know those from whom you learned it, and how from infancy you have known the holy Scriptures, which are able to make you wise for salvation through faith in Christ**

Jesus. All Scripture is God-breathed and is useful for teaching, rebuking, correcting and training in righteousness, so that the man of God may be thoroughly equipped for every good work. (2 Tim. 3:14–17 NIV)

In this passage are two key words, *teaching* and *training*. Teaching is included in training, but it is not quite the same thing. Training involves the will, the desire to do something. But when you teach children, they understand what they should do. Children can be taught the right thing to do, but to make it happen, they must have the will or desire to do what is right. Children may be taught that it is right to save money on a regular basis, but they have not really accomplished anything until they are able to save without any prodding from you.

Training is a long-term process, and the results of training may not show up until the children become adults. Training helps people form the proper habits. So if children are taught the right financial principles from God's Word and are able to demonstrate the use of that knowledge by forming the right financial habits based on that teaching, they will make the right financial decisions and will reap the appropriate rewards that will result in an improved financial lifestyle.

The apostle Paul advised, "Children, obey your parents in the Lord, for this is right. 'Honor your father and mother'—which is the first commandment with a promise—'that it may go well with you and that you may enjoy long life on the earth'" (Eph. 6:1–3 NIV). When we obey God and live our lives according to his Word and then teach our children to do the same, our children receive the same benefits of obedience as we do.

To help your kids, divide money management into five basic areas: earning, giving, saving, spending, and borrowing. In your daily routines while you bank, pump gas, or discuss family vacations, use every opportunity to give clear, practical examples of these principles.

As your kids grow, so should their financial lessons and responsibilities. Whatever your financial philosophy, you can make your kids money-smart.

EARNING

Giving your children a regular allowance remains one of the best tools for helping them learn to manage money. Who is old enough to receive an allowance? Anyone who is old enough to spend, certainly kids age six and older. Consider an allowance as money you're going to spend on your children anyway. An allowance teaches them to distinguish between *needs* and *wants*. When kids control purse strings, money's limitations become real and tangible.

Decide, along with your children, what expenses their allowance will cover, including some for their needs, and some for their wants. Then back off and allow them to make decisions, even poor ones, to help them learn.

GIVING

The children need to know that God owns it all, that we are just stewards. As recognition of that ownership and our faith and trust in God, we give 10 percent, a tithe, back to him. Teaching children to tithe will be an investment that will pay dividends for the rest of their lives.

SAVING

Young children don't really understand the need for stashing money for a rainy day or for postponing pleasures. To help them grasp the concept of saving, try visually demonstrating the rewards.

Tape a picture of an item they want badly, perhaps a toy, to the side of a savings jar. Let them help you deposit your loose change into the jar and once a week add it up. When enough is saved to purchase the item, give the little ones the thrill of carrying the jar to the store and making the purchase themselves. It's a practical way for your children to learn that all money will eventually be spent. Saving is merely spending postponed.

SPENDING

When sitting down to hash out a budget with your youngsters, explain to them that it is a spending plan. Allowing them to understand budgeting could set the tone for a more productive financial life. Start by showing your children a list of household expenses. In fact, make two lists, one showing food, shelter, clothing, and other needs, and another list showing what you spend for movies, concerts, and other wants. Make it clear that good money management means tracking where money comes from and where it goes.

Encourage your children to save at least 10 percent of their allowance or total earnings. By drafting spending plans together, you'll be surprised at the influence you can have in raising money-smart kids.

BORROWING

Even if your children have developed the good habit of saving, in the interest of raising money-smart kids, you should teach them to be savvy borrowers. Some things are difficult to save for, even with a nest egg, for example, a house or car. You are not promoting a buy-now-pay-later mentality by introducing lessons in borrowing.

One way to teach good borrowing habits is to let your children borrow from you, perhaps an advance on their allowance. Set a repayment schedule and charge interest, only pennies for the younger ones.

Point out that when they service debt, their savings stop growing. Your money-smart kids will soon understand that it is a financial option but that borrowing does cost. Also make sure they realize that it should be a last resort and not a way of life.

YOUR WORK LIFE AND MONEY

CORPORATE MANAGERS AND ENTREPRENEURS

With so many Christians in the workplace, the business world should be an environment conducive to serving God and providing for your family. Companies should produce products and services with the highest quality. Customers should always love to do business with the companies and send them additional customers looking for such wonderful companies with which to do business.

Workers at every level in the organization should work hard for their bosses, letting their "light" shine through. As these Christian workers become known for their productivity, loyalty, and commitment to the company, they should advance in the corporate ranks. Other employees should seek them out to learn how they did it. Of course, as followers of Jesus Christ, they would be obligated to share "their secret": how their belief in God has allowed them to prosper. The gospel would then be spread to unbelievers, resulting in many souls won for Christ.

This scenario sounds very appealing, but it is unrealistic. It doesn't reflect what is happening in the real world. When I was working in the financial industry, I can't remember meeting or knowing another Christian at work. Now as a businessman, I know many Christians in the workplace. In addition, I know Christians who own businesses. I am convinced that most of them have a real challenge trying to live out their Christian beliefs in the work environment. I believe it is not because they don't want to; it has more to do with the fact that they have not made the spiritual connection between their work and their service to God. Here are some of the reasons we lack this bridge between our Christian beliefs and the workplace:

No Training in Application of Biblical Workplace Principles

When was the last time you heard a sermon on how to apply your Christian principles to the world of work? I don't want to point an accusing finger at pastors, but most pastors have spent little time in the business world, which hampers their ability to teach on the subject from a personal perspective. Most of us spend almost half our waking hours in the workforce. Certainly more sermons, Sunday school lessons, and Bible studies could reflect our involvement with work and focus on workplace issues.

I believe in the years to come that this imbalance will be corrected. There seems to be a growing trend of individuals who come to the ministry after years in the workplace. These ministers should be able to add their personal work experiences to their sermon messages. But until then, to address this necessity, we need more Christian businessmen and businesswomen who are willing to share their stories and train other employees in ways to reconcile their faith with the world of work.

Letting the World Influence Us

If God's people don't receive adequate training about how to apply our faith to the world of business and work, then we will be more likely to accept the world's view. What is the world's view? The world tells us that we are to cheat, connive, and deceive to get ahead. The end justifies the means. We read about the businessman who is successful but has achieved his accomplishments at the expense of all the people who helped him along the way. We are taught that the world of business is not a place for nice guys because nice guys finish last. To be successful, we should crush the enemy, scorch the earth, and take no prisoners.

The people involved in the world of work who think this way develop a sort of schizophrenia. They act one way at church and another on the job. I remember how I felt when I met a church leader's colleague at a social function. When I told him how involved our mutual friend was at church and how his Christian lifestyle was always admired, the fellow didn't think that we were talking about the same person. The person he knew showed a whole different side to his personality that left his relationship with the Lord sorely lacking.

Some people may be reluctant to act out their Christian beliefs because people who knew them when they were not saved would not accept them any longer. And let's be honest. They don't nail Christians to crosses anymore but an employer who is not a follower of Jesus Christ can make life quite miserable and perhaps have employees wishing they still did. Therefore, too many Christians keep their beliefs to themselves.

Then there are Christians who believe in the "name it and claim it gospel." They maintain if you can conceive it, you can achieve it. To these folks, God is a genie who grants them their every wish. They believe that the only way to measure God's pleasure with them is by their material rewards and worldly success.

Many Christians Think That Work Cannot Be Ministry

I know several church members and friends who, after spending a substantial part of their lives in the corporate world, have enrolled in seminary and subsequently pursued a life in full-time ministry. Although I don't question their desire to be ministers, I am convinced that many of them chose that path because they didn't see their work as ministry. They believed that the only way to serve God was to become a full-time minister. Don't get me wrong. There are probably few activities that deserve our support more than the local church and its ministries. But if we relegate "ministry" to only those who are available through the local church, we confine our ability to properly serve God.

We need more born-again Christians who are willing to stay employed in the workplace. Jesus went where the sinners hung out. The body of Christ needs believers who can make a stand for Christ and serve as role models for those who have lost their way. Many unsaved people may have a tough time walking into a church. But they have to work somewhere, and they have to live somewhere. Sometimes the idea of talking to a pastor can be intimidating. Since society tends to put ministers on a pedestal, fellow workers or neighbors may be more willing to share with someone they think will understand and is more approachable—and that needs to be Christians on the job and in the neighborhood.

Work in and of itself has value as a ministry and should not be limited to witnessing opportunities, and money provided by work can support the local church and other ministry efforts.

The church needs a broader understanding of ministry as well as guidelines for applying that to our day-to-day business activities. Then we can grow and disciple where we are planted.

One result of this view that work cannot be ministry is that many Christians redirect much of their spiritual enthusiasm toward what they consider to be more concrete ministries, such as church service. If we limit our ministry to what can be accomplished only through our religious service and don't include our work in the mix, then we will overlook the impact that Christians can have in the marketplace. If God's people don't strive to excel in the business world, then Christians will be severely underrepresented among the top business leaders. And in my opinion, Christian business leaders have the opportunity to make a great impact on society.

BASIC CHRISTIAN EMPLOYER/OWNER BUSINESS PRINCIPLES

I have always maintained that if you ever want to have your faith challenged, start and manage a business. This is not to suggest that being employed in the workforce isn't a formidable task, but the issues that arise as a result of being a Christian operating a business will challenge you in every facet of your walk with Christ. Of course, the Ten Commandments give us the rules with which we are to live our lives, but there are some biblical principles that business owners, as well as workers, might want to consider.

1. Reflect Christ in Your Business Practices

The desire to follow in Jesus' footsteps always has a cost: "Then Jesus said to his disciples, 'If anyone would come after me, he must deny himself and take up his cross and follow me'" (Matt. 16:24 NIV). Accepting this principle will cost you money. In a society that gets almost a daily share of how devious, deceptive, and manipulative business leaders can be, as a business owner or worker you will have many chances to suffer for the cause of Christ. Honoring your creditors and being fair to your employees and customers are only two elements of Christian behavior.

Let's take honesty, which is applicable to social transactions and/or mutual dealings in the business environment. *Honesty* is basically "the ability to be fair, candid, and truthful":

> *Kings take pleasure in honest lips;*
> *they value a man who speaks the truth.* (Prov. 16:13 NIV)

> *Put away perversity from your mouth;*
> *keep corrupt talk far from your lips.* (Prov. 4:24 NIV)

Being honest sounds straightforward, but oftentimes how we play this out in real-life situations can become delicate.

My radio program, *Your Personal Finance,* is sponsored by advertisers. The program runs on many radio stations around the country. We are required to get affidavits (signed statements) from each radio station verifying that the program ran on that station. Some companies that produce syndicated programs tend to inflate the number of stations running their programs; consequently, when it is time to verify that the stations ran the program, they come up a little short. As a matter of principle, we have never inflated the number of stations, and this honest reporting has cost us money. The more stations we could claim to have running the program, the more money we could charge advertisers.

One day we got a call that a particular advertiser wanted affidavits for all the stations that ran our program. We promptly replied. Later on we found out that we were one of the two programs the advertiser decided to continue sponsoring because we were honest. We had affidavits for all the stations that ran our program. Being truthful about our station list cost us money in the short run, but in the end it made us money because we established a reputation for honesty and fair dealing.

As a Christian in business, you must *honor people to whom you owe money*. A too common business practice is to try to get the money in the door as fast as possible but try to hold on to the money until the last possible minute. In practice, some businesses collect on invoices as soon as they can, but they delay paying creditors until they absolutely must. This point applies to individuals or companies to whom you owe money as well as to creditors who have loaned you merchandise that you are trying to sell:

> *Do not withhold good from those who deserve it,*
> *when it is in your power to act.*
> *Do not say to your neighbor,*
> *"Come back later; I'll give it tomorrow"—*
> *when you now have it with you.* (Prov. 3:27–28
> NIV)

I understand the ups and downs of running a business. But if it is in your power to make sure someone gets paid on time, as you have agreed, then do it. I believe that is what God would have you do. One of the interesting by-products of honoring your creditors is that when hard times come—and they will—you will have someone with a sympathetic ear who will be willing to work out a more flexible repayment term if the need arises.

Whether you are a business owner or a manager, your most important asset walks out the door every day at 5:00 P.M. or whenever the business closes down. You need to be *fair to your employees.* Now this doesn't mean that you give them everything they want or that you treat everyone the same, for example, paying everyone the same wage. I think God requires that we be open, frank, and honest with people. Most issues revolve around pay and benefits when it comes to treating employees fairly. To understand Jesus' thinking on this, consider the parable of the day laborers:

> **For the kingdom of heaven is like a landowner who went out early in the morning to hire men to work in his vineyard. He agreed to pay them a denarius for the day and sent them into his vineyard. About the third hour he went out and saw others standing in the marketplace doing nothing. He told them, "You also go and work in my vineyard, and I will pay you whatever is right." So they went. He went out again about the sixth hour and the ninth hour and did the same thing. About the eleventh hour he went out and found still others standing around. He asked them, "Why have you been standing here all day long doing nothing?" "Because no one has hired us," they answered. He said to them, "You also go and work in my vineyard." When evening came, the owner of the vineyard said to his foreman, "Call the workers and pay them their wages, beginning with the last ones hired and going on to the first." The workers who were hired about the eleventh hour came and each received a denarius. So when those came who were hired first, they expected to receive more. But each one of them also received a denarius. When they received it, they began to grumble against the landowner. "These men who were hired last worked only**

one hour," they said, "and you have made them equal
to us who have borne the burden of the work and the
heat of the day." But he answered one of them,
"Friend, I am not being unfair to you. Didn't you agree
to work for a denarius? Take your pay and go. I want
to give the man who was hired last the same as I gave
you. Don't I have the right to do what I want with my
own money? Or are you envious because I am generous?" So the last will be first, and the first will be last.
(Matt. 20:1–16 NIV)

Obviously in this story, there is perceived unfairness. The
workers got different amounts for doing the same work.
Actually some got the same amount (a denarius was equivalent
to a day's normal salary) for doing the same work, but working
fewer hours.

If you were an employer and hired someone to work a full
day, someone else to work a half day, and a third person to work
a couple of hours, what salary arrangements would you make
with each worker? If you were hired to work a full day, how
would you expect your compensation to compare with that of
someone hired to work fewer hours? Clearly we can disagree on
the answers to these questions. But I think there is one fact we
can agree on. Everyone got what was promised. No one is
forced to work for you. When you deal with employees, give
them what you have promised them. What a great witness for
Christ to be known as a man or woman of your word!

Other than to the employees you hire and the creditors you
owe, your greatest witness is going to be to your customers.
Your clientele will no doubt take you more seriously because
you give them a good product or service at a fair price and you
are a man or woman of your word. To continue to model Christ
in your life you must *treat all customers fairly.*

In all of your business dealings as a Christian, you have to
execute your responsibilities with the utmost integrity. Integrity
comprehends the whole moral character, but it has a special reference to uprightness in mutual dealings and the transfer of
property for others. In other words, your integrity is reflected in

how you conduct yourself in business dealings with employees, creditors, and customers.

2. Find Christian Advisers

I have probably made you a little uncomfortable several times while you have been reading this book. And if I haven't, keep reading, I probably will. If you are a Christian in business, you need to seek the counsel of other Christians who have expertise in the following areas: law, taxes, financial planning, banking, and your specific industry. Granted, many very qualified, knowledgeable non-Christians can supply you the technical help you may need in these areas. But they can't provide the spiritual understanding you may need to help you with decisions.

How can an attorney who doesn't know the Lord respect the fact that you may not want to sue another Christian? How can a non-Christian banker understand a tax return that indicates you give at least 10 percent to your church? That happened to me. I was applying for a working capital loan for one of my businesses, and my banker who is a Christian noted that his boss thought my net worth should have been higher than it was with the income I was making. Granted, I have a decent net worth, but she thought it should be higher. Well, my banker explained that most of my assets are tied up in the business and are reflected in the net worth of my business. In addition, my banker told me that his boss wanted to know why I gave so much to my church. My banker said that wasn't the first time he had to answer that question because, praise God, he had other customers who tithed too. I eventually received the working capital loan, but as you can see, Christians have to be ready to defend their faith to the world.

I don't believe that we should totally dismiss advice from non-Christians, but the Bible is clear on this issue:

> *Blessed is the man*
> *who does not walk in the counsel of the wicked*
> *or stand in the way of sinners*
> *or sit in the seat of mockers.*
> *But his delight is in the law of the LORD,*

and on his law he meditates day and night.
He is like a tree planted by streams of water,
which yields its fruit in season
and whose leaf does not wither.
Whatever he does prospers. (Ps. 1:1–3 NIV)

This admonition is summed up in the first verse: "Blessed is the man who does not walk in the counsel of the wicked . . . or sit in the seat of mockers." The real issue is not to rely on these non-Christian advisers for regular day-to-day decisions: "He who walks with the wise grows wise, / but a companion of fools suffers harm" (Prov. 13:20 NIV).

Let me also point out that we must always measure our advice against God's Word. Be careful about the advice you receive, especially if you cannot find something in Scripture that supports it. Granted, I understand you may not always be able to find a specific verse in the Bible that gives you the answer to your question. All I am saying is that if there is no biblical reference, you must examine the issue all the more carefully. Don't assume that the advice you get from someone in full-time ministry is always right either. Well, I told you I was going to get in trouble. The deciding factor should be a person's commitment to God. I have received great counsel from pastors, but I have also been the recipient of excellent advice from Christians who are not pastors.

A good counselor should not make the decision for you. Instead, a counselor can help you look at the issue objectively and provide a proper rationale so that you can reach the right decision on your own.

Here are some verses to consider when seeking wise counsel:

Plans fail for lack of counsel,
but with many advisers they succeed. (Prov. 15:22 NIV)

Listen to advice and accept instruction,
and in the end you will be wise. (Prov. 19:20 NIV)

The way of a fool is right in his own eyes,
But he who heeds counsel is wise. (Prov. 12:15 NKJV)

Stay away from a foolish man,
   for you will not find knowledge on his lips. (Prov.
14:7 NIV)

The last but not least Christian adviser you should make a part of your team is your spouse. I don't know what it is about women, but they possess an uncanny intuition. Men tend to be more impulsive and independent and prone to make quick decisions. Both perspectives can serve you well in business, no matter whether you are self-employed or you are on someone else's payroll. My wife works with me in my businesses. She is my wife, mother to my children, business partner, and friend. Sometimes depending on what day it is, one has more priority over the others. But primarily she is my helpmate. She and I share a love for the Lord that permeates everything we do. She was there in the beginning when I started the business, working often for short periods of time two jobs while I worked full-time in the business. For a while she became an at-home mom.

At one point I was trying to find an office manager, and I went through several employees trying to find the right one. One day my office manager quit—she wasn't working out anyway—and my wife, Barbara, had to fill in at short notice. She was able to handle the job better than all the others combined. I had resisted her working with me for all the reasons you hear about husband-and-wife teams. Since then, she has served as my office and financial manager, and she does an excellent job. She works fifteen to twenty hours a week, and what she contributes is invaluable. I run new ideas by her before developing them. Working closely together hasn't been easy. We have to limit the amount of time we talk about work at home so we can focus on our relationship too. But her counsel and help are irreplaceable.

If you are married but do not share your business ideas, issues, or concerns with your wife, then you are missing out on an opportunity to be blessed by what God has brought to you. For the Word advises, "Husbands, in the same way be considerate as you live with your wives, and treat them with respect as the weaker partner and as heirs with you of the gracious gift of life, so that nothing will hinder your prayers" (1 Peter 3:7 NIV). If you don't want your prayers hindered, then include your wife in your business life.

3. Provide a Good Product or Service at a Reasonable Price

You may be saying that this biblical principle should be first. You provide a good product, and the world will beat a path to your door. That may be true, but if you don't do the other things, nobody will be back. To experience God's best, you need to give attention to all three items I've noted here.

Nothing reflects more on a company than the product or service that it provides. Sampling a company's product or service will tell you a lot about the people who work there and produce the product or service: "Whatever you do, work at it with all your heart, as working for the Lord, not for men" (Col. 3:23 NIV). When you work for the Lord you will provide the best product possible.

BASIC CHRISTIAN EMPLOYEE BUSINESS PRINCIPLES

The relationship between an employee and an employer must be understood in the context that an employer is in a position of authority. God calls us to honor those in authority positions, whether they be government or political officials or our supervisors:

> **Everyone must submit himself to the governing authorities, for there is no authority except that which God has established. The authorities that exist have been established by God. Consequently, he who rebels against the authority is rebelling against what God has instituted, and those who do so will bring judgment on themselves.** (Rom. 13:1–2 NIV)

Obey your leaders and submit to their authority. They keep watch over you as men who must give an account. Obey them so that their work will be a joy, not a burden, for that would be of no advantage to you. (Heb. 13:17 NIV)

We are to obey people in authority because God has put them in leadership positions. Obviously the assumption here has to be that we are to obey those in authority unless what they ask us to do contradicts the Word of God.

Several issues apply to you as an employee. First, *show up on time.* I am amazed that so many employees can't seem to get to work on time. I define late as one second past the time you are supposed to report. The excuses are numerous: "My bus was late!" "Traffic was terrible!" "The alarm didn't go off!" "I had to make an important stop before coming in!" I believe that habitual lateness is a sign of disobedience. Being late is a result of disrespect for the rules and regulations that govern the work environment. There is an old saying that I will paraphrase: get a jump on the rest of the workers; just show up on time ready to work. Many of the same people who can't seem to show up on time also take long lunches and leave work early. Your employer deserves a good day's work for a good day's wage. Because you show up on time and work your assigned hours, the company will be the beneficiary of your diligence.

Don't steal. It goes without saying that an employee shouldn't steal. But in addition to outright theft of money, there are more subtle forms of thievery. Take, for instance, using the copier to make copies for your Bible study class. Or perhaps taking company property home, such as pens, pencils, notebooks, copy paper, and message pads. Need I go on? Let's not forget stealing time. It's one thing to get a phone call from a spouse, relative, or friend and limit the call to a few minutes. But I have witnessed employees having hour-long discussions.

Dishonesty is at the root of all stealing: "He whose walk is upright fears the LORD, / but he whose ways are devious despises him" (Prov. 14:2 NIV). I heard of one individual who became upset because his boss wouldn't let him study the Bible on company time. That was stealing the employer's time. I am not trying to be picky, but you get the point. You know when you are abusing the phone privileges, long lunches, and the like. If you get permission from your employer, that is a different matter. You should ask your boss whether you can get personal calls and how long the calls can last. Doing that prevents any misunderstandings later on.

Be loyal. I know someone who wanted to start a part-time business, and he decided to work with a company that sold long-distance service to consumers through a multilevel marketing setup. It could be a great opportunity. The problem was that he worked full-time as an account executive for a major long-distance company. Conflict of interest? I think so. How could he be loyal to his full-time employer knowing that he was trying to take away his employer's current and potential customers? If you find that you can no longer be loyal to your company, then leave. If you don't leave, you will probably eventually be fired anyway when your employer finds out.

These basic Christian business principles are not unachievable goals to fantasize about, but indicators of how seriously we believe in our Lord and Savior Jesus Christ, and how far we are willing to carry that cross.

— 11 —

GAMBLING AND LOTTERIES

In August of 1996 President Clinton signed a measure that set up the National Gambling Impact Study Commission. The nine-member commission will conduct a two-year study focusing on the social and economic effects of gambling on state and local governments, individuals, families, and businesses in the United States. The panel will also look at the relationship between crime and gambling as well as the impact of pathological or problem gambling on society. The study will be released in 1999. Some believe the report will provide a wake-up call to the country. Senator Paul Simon, a Democrat from Illinois who sponsored the measure along with Representative Frank Wolf, a Republican from Virginia, said, "The fastest growing industry in the nation is the gambling industry."

Some Christians don't take the issue of gambling seriously because they cannot find an explicit commandment against gambling. However, biblical principles can be applied to gambling, and we will discuss them. Gambling is a form of risk, and it has more spiritual consequences, as we shall see. When you drive your car, you take a risk that you won't be in an accident. When you get in an airplane, you take a risk that it won't crash. When you ride the roller coaster at an amusement park, you take a risk. When you invest your money in real estate, the stock market, or a business, you take a risk. But the issue surrounding gambling has become more complex with the increasing number of casinos, state-run lotteries, and riverboat gambling. Nothing polarizes people more than to talk about gambling. I

will try to give you some biblical guidelines to help you understand what God says, then let you come to a conclusion for
yourself.

GOD ENCOURAGES RISK TAKING

Let's get some basic issues out of the way first. God is not
opposed to wealth and risk taking. Early in the book I highlighted this verse: "Remember the LORD your God, for it is he
who gives you the ability to produce wealth, and so confirms his
covenant, which he swore to your forefathers, as it is today"
(Deut. 8:18 NIV). In this verse it is clear that God gives us the
ability to acquire wealth and makes it part of his covenant.

In addition, read David's words:

Wealth and honor come from you;
*   you are the ruler of all things.*
In your hands are strength and power
*   to exalt and give strength to all.*
Now, our God, we give you thanks,
*   and praise your glorious name.*

**But who am I, and who are my people, that we should
be able to give as generously as this? Everything comes
from you, and we have given you only what comes from
your hand.** (1 Chron. 29:12–14 NIV)

David praised God because he understood that all that he had
came from the Lord.

God delights in our taking risks so that we may acquire
more wealth in order to take care of our families and spread the
gospel. You remember the parable of the talents (Matt.
25:14–30). Jesus told the story of a master who went away for
a while and left various amounts of money with three servants.
Two servants took some risk and invested the money and
received a return. The third servant took no risk by burying the
money. On his return, the master was not very pleased with him,
to say the least. So God encourages our risk-taking and wealth-
building pursuits.

INVESTING IS NOT THE SAME AS GAMBLING

Some people will say that investing is gambling. Nothing could be farther from the truth. With investing, you place your money in the investment and expect a return that is commensurate with the risk you are taking. In the case of most investments it is possible that you will get some or all of your money back if the investment doesn't perform up to expectations. With gambling, someone has to lose for you to win, and the majority of the time, you don't receive any of your money back unless you win. With gambling, there is also the question of motivation. Most people who gamble do so with a get-rich-quick mentality. That is not God's will for our lives: "People who want to get rich fall into temptation and a trap and into many foolish and harmful desires that plunge men into ruin and destruction. For the love of money is a root of all kinds of evil. Some people, eager for money, have wandered from the faith and pierced themselves with many griefs" (1 Tim. 6:9–10 NIV).

But gamblers seem to flock to one area of investing. Gamblers have different appetites from the rest of us when it comes to investments. Some of the preferred areas of the stock market that have attracted the interest of gamblers have been options, commodities, penny stocks, and new stock offerings. These investments are very speculative, and only the most experienced investors should be involved. Gamblers enjoy the anticipation of following the daily activity surrounding these investments. Newspapers, hourly radio and TV reports, and hundreds of periodicals and magazines add excitement in seeking the investment edge. Action is their game. For gamblers, their investment goals are unclear; they are in it for the feeling it gives them as they experience the highs and lows and struggles surrounding the play. When this activity starts to affect their relationship with the Lord, a spouse, the family, or an employer, or it causes financial problems, they have crossed over the line from investing to gambling.

THE IMPACT OF GAMBLING

How does gambling affect our lives?

Gambling questions the sovereign rule of God over our lives. Gambling replaces our trust in God with a devotion to luck and games of chance. If your confidence in God has been replaced by the hope of a lucky chance to win the lottery or win at blackjack, you indeed have a problem. To take legitimate risks through sound investments, insurance on life and property, and other prudent forms of financial planning is to be God's steward. But these risks are not substitutes for trust in God.

The first clear biblical reference to gambling came from Isaiah:

> *But as for you who forsake the LORD*
> *and forget my holy mountain,*
> *who spread a table for Fortune*
> *and fill bowls of mixed wine for Destiny,*
> *I will destine you for the sword,*
> *and you will all bend down for the slaughter;*
> *for I called but you did not answer,*
> *I spoke but you did not listen.*
> *You did evil in my sight*
> *and chose what displeases me.* (Isa. 65:11–12 NIV)

The prophet protested against those who counted on the deities Fortune and Destiny, which were the gods of fate and symbols of good and bad luck. The Israelites were trusting in chance rather than God. The prophet denounced them, for biblical faith elevated the providential care of God and the cult of luck flew in its face. We are to live by God's divine guidance, and that is why we operate by planning and prayer and not by chance and luck.

By displacing God as your Source for all your needs through gambling, you are participating in a form of idolatry: "You shall have no other gods before me" (Ex. 20:3 NIV).

Jesus spoke up about wealth: "Do not store up for yourselves treasures on earth, where moth and rust destroy, and where thieves break in and steal. But store up for yourselves treasures in heaven, where moth and rust do not destroy, and where thieves do not break in and steal. For where your treasure is, there your heart will be also" (Matt. 6:19–21 NIV). To say this another way, you will put your money in what you love. You love the church; you will give to help the cause of Christ. You love your car; you will spend money on it.

Gambling causes us to become greedy, and greed leads to covetousness. The seed for greed is planted by our desire to have what other people have. The insatiable desire for money we do not have, for wealth we did not earn, leads to greedy materialism. Covetousness motivates gambling, and gambling itself feeds covetousness, becoming a vicious cycle. Jesus warned, "Watch out! Be on your guard against all kinds of greed; a man's life does not consist in the abundance of his possessions" (Luke 12:15 NIV).

Greedy people are never content. They always want more. Being greedy has nothing to do with what they have. Greedy people can be rich, middle class, or poor. It has more to do with the lustful desire to have more wealth and more money. A consuming desire to have more will only lead to "temptation and a trap and into many foolish and harmful desires that plunge men into ruin and destruction. For the love of money is a root of all kinds of evil. Some people, eager for money, have wandered from the faith and pierced themselves with many griefs" (1 Tim. 6:9–10 NIV).

God condemns greedy people who are so fond of get-rich-quick schemes. The Bible clearly admonishes us to avoid such ideas:

> **The plans of the diligent lead to profit**
> **as surely as haste leads to poverty.** (Prov. 21:5 NIV)

> **A faithful man will be richly blessed,**
> **but one eager to get rich will not go unpunished.**
> (Prov. 28:20 NIV)

To understand greed, you have to ask yourself, Am I satisfied with what I have? To be content in this way is a blessing from God: "Godliness with contentment is great gain" (1 Tim. 6:6

NIV). To avoid financial traps and schemes, pursue God's plan for your life, stick with what you know, seek good counsel, and wait on God's peace before acting.

Gambling violates the central moral imperative in the Bible—the law of love. When asked about the greatest commandment, Jesus replied, "'Love the Lord your God with all your heart and with all your soul and with all your mind.' This is the first and greatest commandment. And the second is like it: 'Love your neighbor as yourself'" (Matt. 22:37–39 NIV). Love imposes great demands on us. Love leads us to always seek the welfare of our neighbors. How can we love others when they have to lose so that we can win? Most people trying to work out a deal look for a win-win situation. With gambling, especially a lottery, there have to be millions of losers to have just a handful of winners. That is not God's way. That is not love. But that is what gambling is all about.

Love seeks to build others up. Gambling doesn't do that. It appeals to people's weakest instincts. Gambling feeds the thought that the only way they are going to get ahead is to risk their money in a game where the odds are stacked against them. The odds are better that they can flip "heads" on a coin twenty times in a row (one in 524,288) than the odds of winning the Florida lottery (one in 13,983,820). Gambling tries to convince people that they can't better themselves by their own effort, that the state-run lottery or privately or publicly owned casino has a ticket to a brighter future.

Some people say that they gamble because it is fun. Well, I don't buy that. Most people like playing the lottery or the slot machines because it is fun only when they win. Contrast that to people who play a sport because it is fun. They play basketball, football, tennis, or golf because they enjoy disciplining their bodies and minds to accomplish something. If they win, that is great! But if they lose, they still have the enjoyment of having played. With gambling, it is either all or nothing. Win, and they have fun. Lose, and it can be a disaster.

God is not against our having fun: "For he chose us in him before the creation of the world to be holy and blameless in his sight. In love he predestined us to be adopted as his sons through Jesus Christ, in accordance with his pleasure and will" (Eph. 1:4–5 NIV). God wanted us to be adopted as his children because it was his pleasure to do so. He also has tremendous joy when we are doing well:

> *May those who delight in my vindication*
> *shout for joy and gladness;*
> *may they always say, "The LORD be exalted,*
> *who delights in the well-being of his servant.* (Ps. 35:27 NIV)

> *For the LORD takes pleasure in His people;*
> *He will beautify the humble with salvation.* (Ps. 149:4 NKJV)

Fun becomes illegitimate when it crowds God out of our lives. Paul said that the final days will be marked by people who are lovers of themselves and lovers of money, among other things. They will be "lovers of pleasure rather than lovers of God" (2 Tim. 3:4 NIV). Does your gambling crowd God out of your life? Are you able to give to his kingdom as you should, or are you waiting for your "ship" to come in from gambling winnings?

Gambling violates the biblical principle of stewardship of possessions. As Christians, we are called to be good stewards of all God has given us and to use these resources for God's glory and human good. Since everything we have belongs to God, then God is bankrolling our gambling activities. It would appear that gambling is bad stewardship if it means that God can't supply our needs and we must rely on hitting the lucky number at Lotto in order to get what we want. We may look around and think that God has answered everyone else's prayers but our own. Sometimes God's answer is to wait, and we don't know the circumstances of how other people are having their needs met. Satan can make people rich too:

> *Be still before the LORD and wait patiently for him;*
> *do not fret when men succeed in their ways,*
> *when they carry out their wicked schemes.* (Ps. 37:7 NIV)

Gambling can have an adverse effect on our society and community. Gambling destroys Christian influence. As Christians, we are called to abstain from evil and imitate Christ in our lives and actions. Christian influence should be exerted in positive ways to build up community life, not tear it down. What we do seems to have more of an impact on Christian witness than what we say. Our actions can hurt our testimony to others. So, the spiritual effect of gambling is obvious—it can negatively impact our ability to disciple others for Christ. The apostle Paul asserted,

> **Though I am free and belong to no man, I make myself a slave to everyone, to win as many as possible. To the Jews I became like a Jew, to win the Jews. To those under the law I became like one under the law (though I myself am not under the law), so as to win those under the law. To those not having the law I became like one not having the law (though I am not free from God's law but am under Christ's law), so as to win those not having the law. To the weak I became weak, to win the weak. I have become all things to all men so that by all possible means I might save some. I do all this for the sake of the gospel, that I may share in its blessings.**
> (1 Cor. 9:19–23 NIV)

Paul seemed to be saying that sometimes I have to restrict my freedom. I have to be conscious of what I do to keep from undercutting my witness: "Be careful, however, that the exercise of your freedom does not become a stumbling block to the weak" (1 Cor. 8:9 NIV); and "If what I eat causes my brother to fall into sin, I will never eat meat again, so that I will not cause him to fall" (1 Cor. 8:13 NIV).

As we mature in Christ, we learn there are many things that we can do. But some people who are still maturing in Christ or have not yet made the decision to follow Jesus may still be struggling. We don't want our witness to be hampered by actions that we may think are acceptable.

As I have discussed earlier in the book, money is a spiritual issue. Its use or misuse has spiritual consequences. If money isn't used for taking care of family needs and supporting the work of the Lord, then the misuse will have an effect on your spiritual condition. When you gamble, you are diverting money that should be used for these purposes, and that is not God's way. Gambling will have an effect on your spiritual life, not the least of which is your testimony to the unsaved. My belief is that the spiritual effect of using money to gamble leads to the other issues that adversely affect society and the community, and that it can cause you to become addicted, lose the value of work, and question your judgment.

Gambling addiction is real. Paul declared, "'Everything is permissible for me'—but not everything is beneficial. 'Everything is permissible for me'—but I will not be mastered by anything" (1 Cor. 6:12 NIV). People who become addicted to something cannot help themselves. They are out of control, and they are dangerous.

To understand how ridiculous it is to gamble, think about this:

- The odds of winning the California Super Lotto Jackpot are 1 in 18 million.[1]
- The odds of being killed by terrorists while traveling abroad are 1 in 650,000.[2]
- The odds of getting struck by lightning are 1 in 30,000.[3]

How far have we come? Two decades ago, only two states had legal gambling, and forty-eight states outlawed it. Today forty-eight states have some form of legal gambling. Only Hawaii and Utah do not. Here are other interesting gambling statistics:[4]

- More than 60 percent of American adults gambled over the past twelve months on some activity. More than 80 percent say that gambling is legitimate and casinos are okay.
- Gambling generates more revenue than movies, spectator sports, theme parks, cruise ships, and recorded music combined.

- Gambling has become a $40 billion a year industry in the United States.
- From 1974 to 1994, the amount of money Americans legally wagered has risen 2,800 percent, from $17 billion to $482 billion.

GAMBLING AFFECTS ALL OF US

Gambling problems cross all socioeconomic levels, cultures, races, ages, and gender. Four studies of teen gambling behavior in Minnesota between 1990 and 1995 found a majority of teens between the ages of fifteen and eighteen gambling. The following factors are associated with adolescent problem gamblers:[5]

- 83 percent admitted to committing illegal activities.
- 72 percent are regular drug users.
- 75 percent have at least one parent who gambles.
- 60 percent of the adolescents who gamble started by the sixth grade.
- 86 percent of adolescent problem gamblers are male.

Experts believe that gambling has become the fastest-growing teen addiction problem. A 1996 article in *Christianity Today* revealed how a nineteen-year-old youth from a small Iowa town, unable to face his large gambling losses, penned a short note, saying, "I'm out of control." Then he killed himself. Three New Jersey high school students were arrested for running a $6,500 per week sports betting operation. And a sixteen-year-old paid off gambling debts by turning his girlfriend into a prostitute. Gambling is now affecting our future generations.

Theoretically lotteries were intended as a perfect way to raise revenues for needy state and local governments without having to raise taxes and unduly burden the lower class (less-educated and/or less-affluent people). As is often the case, however, the bridge between theory and practice is out of service, especially in regard to lotteries. Rather than providing relief, lotteries burden people least able to pay.

A study conducted in the Detroit, Michigan, area found, among other things, that individuals in the lowest-income group (less than $10,000 per year) spend the same amount annually on lottery tickets as do those in the highest-income group ($70,000 and over per year). The people in the low-income group spend eight times more, as a percentage of income, on the lottery than do those in the high-income group. Similarly persons with less than a high school diploma spend more than five times more, as a percentage of income, on the lottery than do those with at least a college degree.

A 1994 study by Mary Herring and Timothy Bledsoe has shown that the degree of lottery participation is a declining function of income and education, and that participation is higher among black, male, and older respondents. The pressures for finding nontax means of raising revenue need to be balanced with the consensus of research showing that the burden of lottery finance falls heavily on those least able to pay.[6]

"Although low income persons spent fewer absolute dollars, lottery play represented a heavier burden for the poor in that a larger proportion of household expenditures were consumed by purchasing tickets," reported Daniel J. Brown, Dennis O. Kaldenberg, and Beverly A. Browne.

Lotteries are not the benefit to the poor that they were supposed to be. The authors of an Oregon lottery study even suggest that, if not for the voluntary participation factor, lotteries would be a strong example of class conflict theory, how the elite (the affluent and well-educated, i.e., the policy makers) exploit less-advantaged persons.

It is true that no one is forced to play the lottery. However, that does not necessarily mean that no exploitation, in any degree, is taking place. One expert suggests that although no one is literally forcing poor people to gamble, the fact that they see gambling as one of their few opportunities for investing and for transforming their lives—a point of view that governments and the gambling industry often highlight in their promotional campaigns—means their voluntary willingness to gamble represents what might be called the coercion of circumstance, certainly more so than it does for higher-income people.

Casino gambling interests readily agree that state lotteries attract poor and less-educated people. However, casinos, they claim, feed off a higher-class clientele. "Lotteries appeal mainly to the lowest economic levels of society as a way to change their lives," says Michael Rose, CEO of the Promus Companies (the parent corporation of Harrah's Casinos). "On the other hand, casino entertainment is played by well-educated, affluent adults for entertainment."[7]

Frank Fahrenkopf, president and CEO of the American Gaming Association, seems to suggest that only people who can afford it gamble in casinos: "People who can least afford it, if you want to talk about the economic scale, play the state lotteries, they don't travel and go to casinos." From this perspective, casino taxes seem like a good (progressive) way to "take from the rich and give to the poor."[8]

Three professors, Mary O. Borg, Paul M. Mason, and Stephen L. Shapiro, in the Department of Economics at the University of North Florida, gathered data from nearly one thousand casino players and nongamblers in the Las Vegas and Atlantic City areas to determine the regressiveness of taxes on casino gambling. Borg and her associates also looked at how much money individuals in different income categories spend annually toward gambling, in total dollars and as a percentage of income. The findings are very revealing: people earning less than $10,000 per year spend more than two times as much money, as a percentage of income, on gambling than people making $30,000 to 40,000 per year. Compared to people making more than $80,000 per year, those in the $10,000 and less per year category spend four times as much, as a percentage of income, on gambling.

Borg and her associates also concluded, "Those that are least able to afford it" gamble at casinos, too, contrary to what Fahrenkopf indicated. And while some of the "well-educated and affluent" do gamble at casinos, it is clearly wrong to imply that the poor and less-educated do not, as Rose does. Even according to Harrah's figures on casino gamblers, almost 50 percent have no college education (Harrah's does not say how many of those have no high school education), and half make less than $41,000 per year, hardly what I would call the "well-educated and affluent."[9]

GAMBLING DOES NOT LEAD TO ECONOMIC GROWTH

One argument of gambling enthusiasts is that gambling is a valid strategy for economic development. But John Warren Kindt dispels this myth. Kindt is a professor at the University of Illinois at Urbana-Champaign, who authored a report entitled "The Business-Economic Impacts of Licensed Casino Gambling in West Virginia: Short-Term Gain but Long-Term Pain."[10]

Kindt says the reality is that the legalization of gambling activities eventually causes (1) increased taxes, (2) a loss of jobs from the overall region, (3) economic disruption of other businesses, (4) increased crime, and (5) large social-welfare costs for society in general and government agencies in particular.

For example, two studies of the riverboat casinos in Illinois concluded that for every job created by the riverboats, most of the surrounding communities probably lost one or more jobs from preexisting businesses.

In recent economic history, legalized gambling activities have been directly and indirectly subsidized by taxpayers. The field research throughout the nation reveals that for every $1 the legalized gambling interests indicate is being contributed in taxes, it usually costs the taxpayers at least $3—and higher numbers have been calculated.

Terrence Brunner, executive director of the Chicago-based Better Government Association, said surveys by his organization have found that businesspeople in the vicinity of gambling establishments repeatedly told of how visitors to casinos bypassed their businesses. Robert Goodman, an urban planner, economic development consultant, and author, insists that the cost of counseling problem gamblers is minor. The "real costs" are in "how they behave." They borrow money, sell property and other assets they own, and don't pay off their debts. Others write bad checks, then move into fraud and even bankruptcy. The costs are borne by the person, the private economy, and the government.

Studies have done a lot to take away the other arguments for gambling, especially for state-run lotteries: that "giving people the choice to raise money by purchasing lottery tickets would hold the line on taxes and that the benefits of the lottery far exceed the social costs."

GAMBLING DOESN'T HELP OUR SCHOOLS

The final argument is, "We need money if we want good schools. Either we have a huge tax bill or we approve a lottery." Providing money for education is the explicit and implicit promise of many lottery promoters. There is a widespread public perception that lottery revenues are being used to substantially fund education. But according to a *Money* magazine article in 1996, during the last decade, states that claimed to earmark lottery money for education dedicated a declining share of their total spending to schools—despite the growth in lottery revenues.

Florida, for example, reduced school spending from its general revenues, dropping the percentage of the state's budget spent on education from 36 percent in 1990 to 32 percent in 1994. The state created its lottery in 1987 to "enhance education," but the state has simply replaced general revenues with lottery money at a time when student enrollments are increasing.

God made us so that we could be productive. That is evident from the first book of the Bible: "The LORD God took the man and put him in the Garden of Eden to work it and take care of it" (Gen. 2:15 NIV). God made Adam so that even in the Garden of Eden, he was to have a productive and meaningful life through work. God didn't leave it to chance or luck for Adam to have a profitable life. Most people who gamble do so because they are trying to use the game of chance to get things that God wants us to work for. The apostle Paul warned, "He who has been stealing must steal no longer, but must work, doing something useful with his own hands, that he may have something to share with those in need" (Eph. 4:28 NIV).

I believe God wants us to work so that we will have self-esteem and so that our labor will produce excess and we will have something to give to others. Working productively benefits ourselves and others. And God's Word says that if we don't work, we shouldn't eat: "For even when we were with you, we gave you this rule: 'If a man will not work, he shall not eat'" (2 Thess. 3:10 NIV). Harsh perhaps, but very motivating. A lot of people would probably not work if they knew they could get a good meal every day without having to do anything to earn it. That is the problem with many of our social programs. They encourage people to take a handout and to keep taking it.

People who gamble want the easy way out. They want to be lazy. The first thing most people say they will do if they hit the lottery is to stop working. They don't recognize that work is ordained by God and has a purpose in our lives. Most people would go crazy if they didn't have anything to look forward to every day. If you don't believe it, talk to some retired people. After they have spent time doing all the things they said they couldn't do while working, they beg someone to hire them to do something or volunteer their time.

God's Word leaves no doubt about those individuals who desire to be "sluggards":

How long will you lie there, you sluggard?
When will you get up from your sleep?
A little sleep, a little slumber,
    a little folding of the hands to rest—
and poverty will come on you like a bandit
    and scarcity like an armed man. (Prov. 6:9–11 NIV)

Lazy hands make a man poor,
    but diligent hands bring wealth. (Prov. 10:4 NIV)

THE ODDS ARE STACKED AGAINST YOU

Gambling is not a smart way to use your money. The Bible tells us that we should use common sense, understanding, and insight when we make decisions. Earlier you saw the odds of winning at gambling, especially lotteries and casinos. You have a better chance of being struck by lightning or being killed by terrorists. So armed with the facts, do you still gamble? Spending money on gambling is not a wise move. Why? Well, even if we forget the spiritual issues involved, it isn't wise because the odds are stacked against you for winning.

Gambling is not a wise risk. The only risks that are worth taking are those that will support your family or advance the gospel. If you gamble your money, the only way you will get any money back is to win. It is an all-or-nothing proposition. Jesus said, "Suppose one of you wants to build a tower. Will he not first sit down and estimate the cost to see if he has enough money to complete it?" (Luke 14:28 NIV). The cost here is not only your money, but the risk you run in getting addicted and the cost to society and your family. That cost is too high to pay.

When you gamble, you are going for the long shot. Scripture tells us that we should take well-calculated risks, not all-or-nothing gambles that risk everything:

> *By wisdom a house is built,*
> *   and through understanding it is established;*
> *through knowledge its rooms are filled*
> *   with rare and beautiful treasures.* (Prov. 24:3–4 NIV)

Risk taking should not be done without consulting the Lord:

> *Trust in the LORD with all your heart*
> *   and lean not on your own understanding;*
> *in all your ways acknowledge him,*
> *   and he will make your paths straight.* (Prov. 3:5–6 NIV)

And when in doubt about a situation that seems too good to be true, ask a Christian brother or sister for advice: "Plans fail for lack of counsel, / but with many advisers they succeed" (Prov. 15:22 NIV).

Gambling corrupts the God-ordained purpose of state. Jesus urged us to be salt and light: "You are the salt of the earth.

But if the salt loses its saltiness, how can it be made salty again? It is no longer good for anything, except to be thrown out and trampled by men. You are the light of the world. A city on a hill cannot be hidden" (Matt. 5:13–14 NIV). As believers, we are to use moral persuasion and legitimate power to influence society for the common good. The apostle Paul said that the government was designed to do us good: "For he is God's servant to do you good. But if you do wrong, be afraid, for he does not bear the sword for nothing. He is God's servant, an agent of wrath to bring punishment on the wrongdoer" (Rom. 13:4 NIV).

God's purpose is for the state to establish justice. How can God approve any state that uses a basic human weakness (gambling) as a means for collecting taxes, then becomes a sponsor and promoter of the scheme that always pays back less than people have put in? The state becomes so addicted to the income received from the victims that it must promote gambling to keep the revenues coming in.

Seen in the light of God's Word, gambling is personally selfish and morally irresponsible, and it will wreak havoc with our society if we give it enough time.

GAMBLERS ANONYMOUS 20 QUESTIONS

Are you a compulsive gambler?

Only you can decide. In short, compulsive gamblers are those whose gambling has caused continuing problems in any facet of their lives. Most problem gamblers answer yes to at least seven of Gamblers Anonymous's "20 Questions." The following questions may be of help to you:

1. Did you ever lose time from work due to gambling?
2. Has gambling ever made your home life unhappy?
3. Did gambling affect your reputation?
4. Have you ever felt remorse after gambling?
5. Did you ever gamble to get money with which to pay debts or otherwise solve financial difficulties?

6. Did gambling cause a decrease in your ambition or efficiency?

7. After losing did you feel you must return as soon as possible and win back your losses?

8. After a win did you have a strong urge to return and win more?

9. Did you often gamble until your last dollar was gone?

10. Did you ever borrow to finance gambling?

11. Have you ever sold anything to finance gambling?

12. Were you reluctant to use "gambling money" for normal expenditures?

13. Did gambling make you careless of the welfare of yourself and your family?

14. Did you ever gamble longer than you had planned?

15. Have you ever gambled to escape worry or trouble?

16. Have you ever committed, or considered committing, an illegal act to finance gambling?

17. Did gambling cause you to have difficulty in sleeping?

18. Do arguments, disappointments, or frustrations create within you an urge to gamble?

19. Did you ever have an urge to celebrate any good fortune by a few hours of gambling?

20. Have you ever considered self-destruction as a result of your gambling?

Reprinted with permission from Gamblers Anonymous, Inc., Los Angeles, California.

— 12 —

YOUR PRAYER LIFE AND MONEY

In his book *Healing Words,* Larry Dossey highlights the study by cardiologist Randolph Byrd, who is also a Christian. Dr. Byrd designed a study as a scientific evaluation of the role of God in the healing process. Over a ten-month period, a computer assigned 393 patients of a coronary care unit in San Francisco General Hospital either to a group that was prayed for by home prayer groups (192 patients) or to a group that was not remembered in prayer (201 patients). The study was designed according to strict scientific criteria, the kind used in clinical studies in medicine. The groups were asked to pray each day. They were given the first names of their patients as well as brief descriptions of their illness and condition. The doctors, nurses, or patients did not know which group the patients were in. The study yielded the following results for the prayed-for patients:

1. They were five times less likely than the unprayed-for group to require antibiotics (three patients compared to sixteen patients).
2. They were three times less likely to develop pulmonary edema, a condition in which the lungs fill with fluid as a consequence of the failure of the heart to pump properly (six compared to eighteen patients).

3. None of the prayed-for group required endotracheal intubation, in which an artificial airway is inserted in the throat and attached to a mechanical ventilator, while twelve in the unprayed-for group required mechanical ventilatory support.

4. Few patients in the prayed-for group died (although this difference was not statistically significant).

Dossey concludes in his book that if it had been a new drug or a surgical procedure instead of prayer, scientists would have heralded it as a great breakthrough. Even some skeptics of faith-healing, such as Dr. William Nolan, admitted that perhaps doctors ought to be writing on their order sheets, "Pray three times a day."

In 1996 the Harvard Medical School released a survey of physicians revealing that 99 percent of them feel that belief in God can contribute to healing. In addition, 80 percent think that prayer and meditation are beneficial and should be taught in medical schools.

It is interesting to observe the medical and scientific community learning to embrace what we Christians already know. Those of us who are disciples of Jesus don't need scientific proof because our personal relationship with Jesus Christ is testimony in and of itself that prayer works!

WHAT IS PRAYER?

Prayer is communication with God. To communicate with someone, you must have a relationship with him or her. So to communicate with God, you must have a relationship with him. As you talk to God, you develop a deeper, richer relationship, and as you develop that relationship, God changes you. Spending time with someone ensures that the person's character and personality will influence you. That's why the Bible discusses being on guard about the company you keep:

> *Blessed is the man*
> *who does not walk in the counsel of the wicked*
> *or stand in the way of sinners*

> *or sit in the seat of mockers.*
> *But his delight is in the law of the LORD,*
>   *and on his law he meditates day and night.*
> *He is like a tree planted by streams of water,*
>   *which yields its fruit in season*
> *and whose leaf does not wither.*
>   *Whatever he does prospers.* (Ps. 1:1–3 NIV)

Spend a while with your kids, and you start injecting more slang into your vocabulary. As your kids spend more time with you, they start talking like an adult (I hope).

Prayer is getting to know the mind of God. To know the mind of God is to know God's will for your life. Once you know God's will for your life, everything else that you do will flow from that realization. You will know what job you should have, where you should live, the person you should marry, how to raise your kids and, of course, what to do with your money.

We have already established that God owns it all and that every spending decision is in reality a spiritual decision. There is nothing more or less spiritual about giving a tithe than spending money on a vacation. If it is all God's money to begin with, then implicitly whenever you make a spending decision, you are saying that this is what God would have you do with his resources. That frees you to use God's resources for the accomplishment of the goals and desires that God places in your heart, with no guilt feelings. All of this implies that you are listening to God on a regular basis to determine what he would have you do with his resources. Prayer comes in at this point. One of the best ways to ensure that you hear from God on a regular basis is to pray.

YOUR PART

When it comes to getting answers to prayers, some things are your responsibility and other things are God's.

Your part is to speak to God and then put yourself in a position to listen. More specifically your part is to ask, seek, and knock: "*Ask* and it will be given to you; *seek* and you will find; *knock* and the door will be opened to you. For everyone who asks receives; he who seeks finds; and to him who knocks, the door will be opened" (Matt. 7:7–8 NIV, emphasis added). Understand that you must be a believer in Jesus Christ, for these verses refer to those asking within the "narrow gate": "Enter through the narrow gate. For wide is the gate and broad is the road that leads to destruction, and many enter through it. But small is the gate and narrow the road that leads to life, and only a few find it" (Matt. 7:13–14 NIV); and "If you believe, you will receive whatever you ask for in prayer" (Matt. 21:22 NIV).

The narrow gate is a way of decision, commitment, and obedience to God. You have to believe that Jesus Christ was born of the Virgin Mary, walked this earth, died and was buried, and then rose again on the third day. You have to believe in your heart that the Bible is the inspired Word of God: "If you *remain in me* and *my words remain in you,* ask whatever you wish, and it will be given you" (John 15:7 NIV, emphasis added). By *asking,* you are showing that you depend on God. Your *seeking* suggests yearning and your *knocking* suggests persistence or perseverance. Let's examine these three issues individually.

In addition to being a Christian, the other prerequisite for any request from God is very simple—you have to ask: "You want something but don't get it. You kill and covet, but you cannot have what you want. You quarrel and fight. You do not have, *because you do not ask God*" (James 4:2 NIV, emphasis added); and "At Gibeon the LORD appeared to Solomon during the night in a dream, and God said, '*Ask* for whatever you want me to give you'" (1 Kings 3:5 NIV, emphasis added). That sounds simple enough. So why don't you receive what you ask for? The answer to that is simple also: "When you ask, you do not receive, because you ask with *wrong motives,* that you may spend what you get on your pleasures" (James 4:3 NIV, emphasis added). Oh, boy! Isn't that the truth? You may have selfish motives, reasons, or intentions for wanting a specific financial need met. You may not seek God's will. You may seek to impress neighbors, friends, coworkers, and relatives.

Many people believe that the only requests that God wants to hear about are the big needs, but that was not what Paul said: "Do not be anxious about anything, but in everything, by prayer and petition, with thanksgiving, present your requests to God" (Phil. 4:6 NIV). That means you should pray about everything:

- Financial goals
- Budgets
- Homes
- Cars
- Investments
- Businesses
- Vacations
- Retirement
- Jobs

God doesn't want you to worry about what you ask for in prayer. Paul wrote in Philippians 4:6 before the directive to pray about everything: "Do not be anxious about anything." In others words, don't worry or be afraid, panicky, or apprehensive. God offers a better way. Through Jesus, he said, "So do not worry, saying, 'What shall we eat?' or 'What shall we drink?' or 'What shall we wear?'" (Matt. 6:31 NIV). What did he say you should replace that worry with? "Seek first his kingdom and his righteousness, and all these things will be given to you as well" (Matt. 6:33 NIV).

These other verses have given me encouragement as I *ask* God to answer my prayers: "I will do *whatever you ask in my name,* so that the Son may bring glory to the Father. You may ask me for anything in my name, and I will do it" (John 14:13–14 NIV); and "You did not choose me, but I chose you and appointed you to go and bear fruit—fruit that will last. Then the Father will give you *whatever you ask in my name*" (John 15:16 NIV).

God wants you to *seek* him out in prayer. And when you seek something, you are looking for it, pursuing it, and following it. Seeking suggests you are yearning to hear from God: "Look to the LORD and his strength; / seek his face always" (1 Chron. 16:11 NIV).

Why does God want you to seek him? He loves you and wants you to have a desire for him because he knows he has the answers you are looking for: "I love those who love me, / and those who seek me find me" (Prov. 8:17 NIV). God knows that only through him can you achieve true success. Read farther on in Proverbs 8:

> *With me are riches and honor,*
> > *enduring wealth and prosperity.*
> *My fruit is better than fine gold;*
> > *what I yield surpasses choice silver.*
> *I walk in the way of righteousness,*
> > *along the paths of justice,*
> *bestowing wealth on those who love me*
> > *and making their treasuries full.* (Prov. 8:18–21 NIV)

If that isn't enough to make you seek God for answers to your financial questions, I don't know what would be enough.

Choosing to seek and follow God's wisdom lets you see wealth in the proper perspective, so seeking wealth does not become an all-consuming life goal. God knows that the closer you get to him, what you think are life's goals may change. You may not always get what you ask for. God knows best. Jesus prayed three times for the cup to be removed: "My Father, if it is possible, let this cup pass from Me; nevertheless, not as I will, but as You will" (Matt. 26:39 NKJV). Jesus did not demand its removal, and it was not removed. But he did receive the strength to drink it. Prayer voices human desires but seeks God's perfect will and guidance above all else.

God calls you to continue to *knock* at his door. When you pray, you are to pray without ceasing. You are to be persistent. Jesus told many parables, one of which was to show that "they should always pray and not give up" (Luke 18:1 NIV). In another parable (Luke 11:5–13), the focus was again on persistence. Because of the man's boldness, literally "shamelessness," the friend in the parable finally responded and gave his friend what he was seeking. Prayer should not be curtailed by fear, pride, or shame. You can trust God to accept your boldness. Your persistence validates the reality of your faith. You would not continue to ask God if you didn't believe in him.

The apostles continued to pray for guidance: "They all joined together constantly in prayer, along with the women and

Mary the mother of Jesus, and with his brothers" (Acts 1:14 NIV). Paul wrote, "Be joyful always; pray continually; give thanks in all circumstances, for this is God's will for you in Christ Jesus" (1 Thess. 5:16–18 NIV); and "Pray in the Spirit on all occasions with all kinds of prayers and requests. With this in mind, be alert and always keep on praying for all the saints" (Eph. 6:18 NIV).

James stated, "Perseverance must finish its work so that you may be mature and complete, not lacking anything" (James 1:4 NIV). Your steady and consistent prayer highlights your persistence and represents a victory over circumstances. By achieving this victory, you develop faith in Jesus. By developing faith you will not be tempted to fall back on human experience that denies God and his power.

Human wisdom based on experience is not sufficient to meet life's storms and trials. Believers trust God to provide the needed wisdom and answers to prayer. The need for persistent prayer is not because God is reluctant to give but because we need to be conditioned to receive: "For everyone who asks receives; he who seeks finds; and to him who knocks, the door will be opened" (Luke 11:10 NIV).

You may not always receive what you request. You may not find what you are seeking and the door upon which you knock may not be the one opened, but you have the assurance that where there is asking, there will be receiving; where there is seeking, there will be finding; and where there is knocking, God will open a door.

GOD'S PART

God's part in your prayer life is to listen and to answer in a manner that will bring about your highest good and God's greatest glory. As you get to know God's will for your life, you begin to change and to conform more to the character and person of Jesus Christ. Since all money decisions are spiritual decisions, it is important to know what God would have you do with his resources here on earth. When this happens, all your decisions become easier, including the financial ones.

Work
Sheets

GOALS AND OBJECTIVES

SHORT-TERM (within one year)

GOAL: _____

OBJECTIVE	TIME FRAME	DOLLAR AMOUNT	WEEKLY AMOUNT
_____	_____	$ _____	$ _____
_____	_____	$ _____	$ _____
_____	_____	$ _____	$ _____
_____	_____	$ _____	$ _____
_____	_____	$ _____	$ _____

MEDIUM-TERM (one to four years)

GOAL: _____

OBJECTIVE	TIME FRAME	DOLLAR AMOUNT	WEEKLY AMOUNT
_____	_____	$ _____	$ _____
_____	_____	$ _____	$ _____
_____	_____	$ _____	$ _____
_____	_____	$ _____	$ _____
_____	_____	$ _____	$ _____

LONG-TERM (five or more years)

GOAL: _____

OBJECTIVE	TIME FRAME	DOLLAR AMOUNT	WEEKLY AMOUNT
_____	_____	$ _____	$ _____
_____	_____	$ _____	$ _____
_____	_____	$ _____	$ _____
_____	_____	$ _____	$ _____
_____	_____	$ _____	$ _____

FIGURE 1

PERSONAL BALANCE SHEET

ASSETS

Cash on Hand _____
Checking Account _____
Savings Account _____

Loans Receivable _____

Cash Value Life Insurance _____

Investment Real Estate _____

Personal Residence _____

INVESTMENTS _____
(Market Value)

Stocks _____
Bonds _____
Mutual Funds _____
Certificates of Deposit _____
Retirement Plan (vested interest) _____
IRAs _____
Other _____

PERSONAL PROPERTY
(Present Value)

Home Furnishings _____
Appliances _____
Clothing _____
Jewelry _____
Automobiles _____
Other _____

TOTAL ASSETS _____

LIABILITIES

Current Debts _____
Credit Cards _____
Auto Loans _____

MORTGAGES

Investment Real Estate _____

Personal Residence _____

Home Equity _____

OTHER LIABILITIES

_____ _____
_____ _____
_____ _____
_____ _____

TOTAL LIABILITIES _____

NET WORTH
(assets minus liabilities) _____

FIGURE 2

MONTHLY BUDGET OF INCOME
AND EXPENSES

Income	Budget	Actual	Difference
Salary			
Spouse			
Other			
TOTAL INCOME			

Less Taxes
Federal			
State			
City			
FICA			
Tithe/giving (10%)			
NET INCOME			

Housing (30%)
Mortgage (rent)			
Insurance			
Taxes			
Electricity			
Gas			
Water			
Sanitation			
Telephone			
Maintenance			
Other			
TOTAL HOUSING			

Food (12%)

Automobiles (15%)
Car payments			
Gasoline & oil			
Insurance			
Licenses			
Taxes			
Maintenance & repair			
TOTAL AUTOMOBILES			

Insurance (5%)
Life			
Health			
Other			
TOTAL INSURANCE			

Debts *(5%)*	**Budget**	**Actual**	**Difference**
Credit cards			
Bank loans			
Other			
TOTAL DEBTS			

Entertainment/Recreation *(5%)*

Restaurants			
Travel			
Baby-sitters			
Vacation			
Activities			
Other			
TOTAL ENT./REC.			

Clothing *(5%)*			
Savings *(10%)*			

Medical Expenses *(5%)*

Doctor			
Dentist			
Drugs			
Other			
TOTAL MEDICAL EXP.			

Miscellaneous *(8%)*

Child care			
Beauty/barber			
Laundry/dry cleaning			
Allowances			
Subscriptions			
Gifts			
Education			
Other			
TOTAL MISC.			

TOTAL EXPENSES			

INCOME vs. EXPENSES

NET INCOME			
LESS EXPENSES			
SURPLUS (DEFICIT)			

FIGURE 3

LIST OF DEBTS

Creditor	Type of Loan	Date of Last Payment	Maturity	Monthly Payment $	Total Amount Due $

Total Monthly Payments $ _____

*Total Amount Owed $*_____

Figure 4

FIGURE 5

UPDATED CREDIT PROFILE

EQUIFAX CREDIT INFORMATION SERVICES
The Information Source

The Name and Address of the Equifax office you should contact if you have any questions or disagreement with your credit report

EQUIFAX SAMPLE REPORT OFFICE
BUSINESS ADDRESS
CITY, STATE 00000
PHONE NUMBER

Sample Credit Report

Please address all future correspondence to the address shown on right.

JOHN DOE
123 HOME ADDRESS
CITY, STATE 00000

DATE 06/04/91
SOCIAL SECURITY NUMBER 123-45-6789
DATE OF BIRTH 12/01/60
SPOUSE JANE

I.D. Section
Your name, current address and other identifying information reported by your creditors.

The first item identifies the business that is reporting the information.

CREDIT HISTORY

This is your account number with the company reporting.

This is the month and year you opened the account with the credit grantor.

See explanation below

Number of months account payment history has been reported.

This is the date of last activity on the account and may be the date of last payment or the date of last charge.

The highest amount charged or the credit limit.

Represents number of installments (M=Months) or monthly payment.

The amount owed on the account at the time it was reported.

This figure indicates any amount past due at the time the information was reported.

Date of last account update.

(See explanation below)

Company Name	Account Number	Whose Acct.	Date Opened	Months Reviewed	Date Of Last Activity	High Credit	Terms	Balance	Past Due	Status	Date Reported
SEARS	11251514	I	05/86	66	10/91	3500		0		R1	12/91
C&S	2953900001004731	I	11/86	48	11/90	9388	48M	0		I1	11/90
AMEX	315541125511	I	06/87	24	10/91	500		0		O1	12/91
FNB	54229778	I	05/85	48	10/91	5000	340	3000	680	R3	12/91

>>> PRIOR PAYING HISTORY – 30(03) 60(04) 90+(01) 08/90-R2, 02/89-R3, 10/88-R4 <<<

Number of times account was either 30/60/90 days past due.

Date two most recent delinquencies occurred plus date of most severe delinquency.

Credit History Section
List of open and paid accounts indicating any late payments reported by your creditors.

COLLECTION ACCOUNTS

>>> COLLECTION REPORTED 06/90, ASSIGNED TO PRO COLL 09/89, CLIENT-ABC HOSP AMOUNT-$978, UNPAID 06/90, BALANCE-$978 09/90
DATE OF LAST ACTIVITY 09/89, INDIVIDUAL, ACCOUNT NUMBER 787652IC

Collection Accounts
Accounts which your creditors turned over to a collection agency.

COURTHOUSE RECORDS

>>> LIEN FILED 03/88, FULTON CTY, CASE NUMBER-32114, AMOUNT-$26667, CLASS-CITY/COUNTY RELEASED 07/88, VERIFIED 09/90

>>> BANKRUPCTY FILED 12/89, FULTON CTY, CASE NUMBER-673HC12, LIABILITIES-$15787, PERSONAL INDIVIDUAL, DISCHARGED, ASSETS-$780

Courthouse Records
Public Record items obtained from local, state and federal courts which reflect your history of meeting financial obligations.

AMOUNT-$6904, PLAINTIFF-ABC REAL ESTATE, SATISFIED 03/89, VERIFIED 05/90

ADDITIONAL INFORMATION

>>>FORMER ADDRESS 456 JUPITER, RD, ATLANTA, GA 30245

>>>FORMER ADDRESS P. O. BOX 2138, SAVANNAH, GA 31406

>>>CURRENT EMPLOYMENT ENGINEER, SPACE PATROL

INQUIRY SECTION

·········· COMPANIES THAT REQUESTED YOUR CREDIT HISTORY ··········

06/04/91	EQUIFAX	06/03/90	GECC	08/30/89	MACYS
05/03/91	VISA	04/01/90	FIRST NATL	07/03/89	RICHS
02/13/91	SEARS	03/05/90	PRM VISA	06/20/91	C&S
01/23/91	JC PENNEY	01/03/90	SPEIGEL	06/03/91	FAMILY FIN

INQUIRIES NOT REPORTED TO CUSTOMERS

A PRM inquiry means that only your name and address were given to a credit grantor so they could offer you an application for credit.

An A/M or AR inquiry indicates a periodic review of your credit history by one of your creditors.

An Equifax inquiry indicates our activity in response to your request for a copy of your credit report.
PRM, AM, AR and Equifax inquiries do not show on credit reports that businesses receive, only on reports provided to you.

Status

Type Of Account
O = Open
    (entire balance due
    each month)
R = Revolving
    (payment amount variable)
I = Installment
    (fixed number of payments)

Timeliness Of Payment
0 = Approved not used
1 = Paid as agreed
2 = 30 days past due
3 = 60 days past due
4 = 90 days past due
5 = 120 days past due

7 = Making regular payments
    under wage earner plan
    or similar arrangement
8 = Repossesion
9 = Seriously delinquent/bad
    debt (paid or unpaid)

Length Of Time Information Remains In Your File

Credit and collection accounts— 7 years from date of last activity with original creditor.
Courthouse records— 7 years from date filed except Bankruptcy chapters 7 and 11
    which remain for 10 years from date filed.

Note: New York State only. Satisfied judgments 5 years from the date filed. Paid collections 5
years from date of last activity with original creditor.

Additional Information

Primarily consists of former addresses and employments reported by your creditors.

Inquiry Section

List of businesses that have received your credit report in the last 24 months.

Whose Account

Indicates who is responsible for the account and the type of participation you have with the account.
J = Joint
I = Individual
U = Undesignated
A = Authorized user
T = Terminated
M = Maker
C = Co-Maker/Co-Signer
B = On behalf of another
    person
S = Shared

Form 101089R—1-92 USA

Time is an element we cannot control, other than to start saving now. Answer this question: Who do you think would accumulate more by age sixty-five? A person who started to save $1,000 a year at age twenty-one, saved for eight years, and then completely stopped? Or a person who saved $1,000 a year for thirty-seven years who started at age twenty-nine? Both earned 10 percent on their savings. Is it the person who

	Individual A		Individual B	
Age	Contribution	Year-end Value	Contribution	Year-end Value
21	1,000	1,100	0	0
22	1,000	2,310	0	0
23	1,000	3,641	0	0
24	1,000	5,105	0	0
25	1,000	6,716	0	0
26	1,000	8,487	0	0
27	1,000	10,436	0	0
28	1,000	12,579	0	0
29	0	13,837	1,000	1,100
30	0	15,221	1,000	2,310
31	0	16,743	1,000	3,641
32	0	18,417	1,000	5,105
33	0	20,259	1,000	6,716
34	0	22,284	1,000	8,487
35	0	24,513	1,000	10,436
36	0	26,964	1,000	12,579
37	0	29,661	1,000	14,937
38	0	32,627	1,000	17,531
39	0	35,889	1,000	20,384
40	0	39,478	1,000	23,523
41	0	43,426	1,000	26,975
42	0	47,769	1,000	30,772
43	0	52,546	1,000	34,950
44	0	57,800	1,000	39,545
45	0	63,580	1,000	44,599
46	0	69,938	1,000	50,159
47	0	76,932	1,000	56,275
48	0	84,625	1,000	63,003
49	0	93,088	1,000	70,403
50	0	103,397	1,000	78,543
51	0	112,636	1,000	87,497
52	0	123,898	1,000	97,347
53	0	136,290	1,000	108,182
54	0	149,919	1,000	120,100
55	0	164,911	1,000	133,210
56	0	181,402	1,000	147,631
57	0	199,542	1,000	163,494
58	0	219,496	1,000	180,943
59	0	241,446	1,000	200,138
60	0	265,590	1,000	221,252
61	0	292,149	1,000	244,477
62	0	321,364	1,000	270,024
63	0	353,501	1,000	298,127
64	0	388,851	1,000	329,039
65	0	427,736	1,000	363,043

Total Investment $8,000
Total Amount Accumulated $427,736

Total Investment $37,000
Total Amount Accumulated $363,043

FIGURE 6

PREPARING FOR INVESTMENT

CASH RESERVE FUND

PURPOSE: To have savings equal to six months of your expenses invested in cash or its equivalent.

GOALS: Very safe. Guaranteed rate of return. Easily converted to cash (easy to withdraw).

PORTFOLIO MIX: Three months' expenses invested in safe, interest-bearing account.

Examples: Insured money market account

Three months' expenses invested in cash equivalents

Certificates of deposit or Treasury bills that mature in three months

LIQUIDITY RESERVE

PURPOSE: To provide a second level of security by having 5 percent of your net worth or an additional six months' expenses invested. Willing to assume a slightly higher degree of risk in exchange for a higher return on your money.

GOALS: Want a higher yield than in cash reserve fund. Will accept higher degree of risk. Easily converted to cash.

PORTFOLIO MIX: Diversification is the key. Money allocated depending upon risk tolerance.

Examples: Mutual funds—bond or stock funds

Stocks rated A or better

Bonds rated BBB or better

OPTIONAL INVESTMENT FUND

PURPOSE: To invest in higher yielding and riskier investments that will produce greater investment results.

GOALS: Looking for investments with higher returns. Want to take a more aggressive stance with investments.

PORTFOLIO MIX: Diversification is important. Allocate money depending on risk tolerance.

Examples: Aggressive growth mutual funds

Aggressive growth stocks

High-yield bond funds

High-yield bonds

Gold

Real Estate

Collectibles

Owning a business

FIGURE 7

TAX-EQUIVALENT YIELD CALCULATOR

Directions	Your Calculation	Example
1. Enter the tax-free yield.	_____%	6.0%
2. Subtract your federal tax bracket, expressed as a decimal, from 1.00.	$1.00 - .\underline{\quad} = .\underline{\quad}$	$1.00 - .28 = .72$
3. Divide the tax-free yield (line 1) by line 2 to find the taxable-equivalent yield.	$\underline{\quad} = \underline{\quad}$ %	$\dfrac{6.0}{.72} = 8.33\%$

FIGURE 8

QUICK RETIREMENT PLANNER

<u>Example</u>

Annual income _____ <u>$30,000</u>
Line 1

Years to retirement _____ <u>30</u>
Line 2

Inflation rate _____ <u>6%</u>
Line 3

Amount needed to maintain current _____ <u>$19,500</u>
standard of living (multiply **Line 4**
line 1 x .65)

Current annual income adjusted for _____ <u>$111,988</u>
inflation (multiply line 4 x inflation **Line 5**
multiplier; see figure 10 and use
inflation rate from line 3)

Projected rate of return at retirement _____ <u>.10</u>
(what you anticipate at retirement **Line 6**
your lump sum will earn, expressed
as decimal, i.e., 10% = .10)

Total lump sum retirement needed _____ <u>$1,119,885</u>
(divide line 5 by line 6) **Line 7**

FIGURE 9

ADJUSTING TODAY'S ESTIMATED RETIREMENT NEEDS FOR TOMORROW'S INFLATION

Assumed Rates of Inflation

Years to Go	6%	7%	8%	9%	10%	12%	14%	15%	16%
1	1.060	1.070	1.080	1.090	1.100	1.120	1.140	1.150	1.160
2	1.124	1.145	1.166	1.186	1.210	1.254	1.300	1.322	1.346
3	1.191	1.225	1.260	1.295	1.331	1.405	1.482	1.521	1.561
4	1.262	1.311	1.360	1.412	1.464	1.574	1.689	1.749	1.811
5	1.338	1.403	1.469	1.539	1.611	1.762	1.925	2.011	2.100
6	1.419	1.501	1.587	1.677	1.772	1.974	2.195	2.313	2.436
7	1.504	1.606	1.714	1.828	1.949	2.211	2.502	2.660	2.826
8	1.594	1.718	1.851	1.993	2.144	2.476	2.853	3.059	3.278
9	1.689	1.838	1.999	2.172	2.358	2.773	3.252	3.518	3.803
10	1.791	1.967	2.159	2.367	2.594	3.106	3.707	4.046	4.411
11	1.898	2.105	2.332	2.580	2.853	3.479	4.226	4.652	5.117
12	2.012	2.252	2.518	2.813	3.138	3.893	4.818	5.380	5.926
13	2.133	2.410	2.720	3.066	3.452	4.363	5.092	6.153	6.886
14	2.261	2.579	2.937	3.342	3.797	4.887	6.261	7.076	7.995
15	2.397	2.759	3.172	3.642	4.177	5.474	7.138	8.137	9.266
16	2.540	2.952	3.426	3.970	4.595	6.130	8.137	9.358	10.758
17	2.693	3.159	3.700	4.328	5.054	6.866	9.276	10.761	12.468
18	2.854	3.380	3.996	4.717	5.560	7.690	10.575	12.375	14.463
19	3.026	3.617	4.316	5.142	6.116	8.613	12.056	14.232	16.777
20	3.207	3.870	4.661	5.604	6.728	9.646	13.743	16.367	19.461
25	4.292	5.427	6.848	8.623	10.835	17.000	26.462	32.919	40.874
30	5.743	7.612	10.063	13.268	17.449	29.960	50.950	66.212	85.850

FIGURE 10

HOW RETIREMENT PLAN
ACCUMULATIONS WORK OUT

Age	Total Deposit at Age 65 (at $2,000/yr.)	Rate of Return		
		8%	10%	12%
30	$70,000	$413,126	$700,122	$1,216,042
35	$60,000	$266,846	$413,487	$653,950
40	$50,000	$169,331	$240,826	$347,996
45	$40,000	$104,323	$136,819	$181,462
50	$30,000	$ 60,987	$ 74,167	$ 90,815
55	$20,000	$ 32,097	$ 36,428	$ 41,475
60	$10,000	$ 12,839	$ 13,694	$ 14,618

Double the dollar figures for a married couple (if both work) who contribute $4,000 annually.

FIGURE 11

SOCIAL SECURITY ADMINISTRATION

Request for Earnings and Benefit Estimate Statement

To receive a free statement of your earnings covered by Social Security and your estimated future benefits, all you need to do is fill out this form. Please print or type your answers. When you have completed the form, fold it and mail it to us.

1. Name shown on your Social Security card:

   _____ _____ _____
   First   Middle Initial   Last

2. Your Social Security number as shown on your card:

   ☐ ☐ ☐ – ☐ ☐ – ☐ ☐ ☐ ☐

3. Your date of birth: _____   _____   _____
                        Month   Day   Year

4. Other Social Security numbers you have used:

   ☐ ☐ ☐ – ☐ ☐ – ☐ ☐ ☐ ☐

   ☐ ☐ ☐ – ☐ ☐ – ☐ ☐ ☐ ☐

5. Your Sex: ☐ Male   ☐ Female

6. Other names you have used (including a maiden name):

   _____

   _____

7. Show your actual earnings for last year and your estimated earnings for this year. Include only wages and/or net self-employment income covered by Social Security.

   A. Last year's actual earnings:

   $ ☐ ☐ ☐ , ☐ ☐ ☐ . 0 0
     Dollars only

   B. This year's estimated earnings:

   $ ☐ ☐ ☐ , ☐ ☐ ☐ . 0 0
     Dollars only

8. Show the age at which you plan to retire: ☐ ☐

   (Show only one age)

Form SSA-7004-SM-OP1 (9-91) Destroy prior editions

9. Below, show the average yearly amount that you think you will earn between now and when you plan to retire. Your estimate of future earnings will be added to those earnings already on our records to give you the best possible estimate.

   Enter a yearly average, not your total future lifetime earnings. Only show earnings covered by Social Security. Do not add cost-of-living, performance or scheduled pay increases or bonuses. The reason for this is that we estimate retirement benefits in today's dollars, but adjust them to account for average wage growth in the national economy.

   However, if you expect to earn significantly more or less in the future due to promotions, job changes, part-time work, or an absence from the work force, enter the amount in today's dollars that most closely reflects your future average yearly earnings.

   Most people should enter the same amount that they are earning now (the amount shown in 7B).

   Your future average yearly earnings:

   $ ☐☐☐ , ☐☐☐ . 0 0
   Dollars only

10. Address where you want us to send the statement:

   Name

   Street Address (Include Apt. No., P.O. Box, or Rural Route)

   City   State   Zip Code

   I am asking for information about my own Social Security record or the record of a person I am authorized to represent. I understand that if I deliberately request information under false pretenses I may be guilty of a federal crime and could be fined and/or imprisoned. I authorize you to send the statement of earnings and benefit estimates to the person named in item 10 through a contractor.

   ▶

   Please sign your name (Do not print)

   Date   (Area Code) Daytime Telephone No.

   ABOUT THE PRIVACY ACT
   Social Security is allowed to collect the facts on this form under Section 205 of the Social Security Act. We need them to quickly identify your record and prepare the earnings statement you asked us for. Giving us these facts is voluntary. However, without them we may not be able to give you an earnings and benefit estimate statement. Neither the Social Security Administration nor its contractor will use the information for any other purpose.

FIGURE 12

QUICK LIFE INSURANCE PLANNER

1. Family yearly expenses (including
   yearly amounts set aside for
   retirement and college funds) $50,000
   Line 1

2. Family's yearly income from
   __Social Security   0
   __Spouse's job $30,000
   __Other income   0

                                TOTAL $30,000
                                Line 2

3. Family's investment income
   3a. Total amount of savings/
       investments $5,000
   3b. Interest rate that capital
       would earn (i.e., 6% = .06)   .06

                        Result:
   Family's income from savings and $300
   investments (multiply line 3a by 3b) **Line 3**

4. Shortfall from budget $19,700
   (subtract lines 2 & 3 from   **Line 4**
   line 1)

5. Divide line 4 by 12 $1,642
                                   Line 5

6. Divide 12 by line 3b $200
   (what capital can earn expressed **Line 6**
   as a decimal—i.e., 6% = .06)

7. Total life insurance needed $328,400
   (multiply line 6 by line 5)   **Line 7**

FIGURE 13

THE MOST YOU SHOULD PAY FOR
TERM INSURANCE

Age	*Nonsmokers* Annual Premium* Male	Female	Age	*Smokers* Annual Premium* Male	Female
18–30	$ .76	$ .68	18–30	$ 1.05	$ 1.01
31	.76	.69	31	1.10	1.05
32	.77	.70	32	1.15	1.10
33	.78	.71	33	1.21	1.15
34	.79	.72	34	1.28	1.20
35	.80	.74	35	1.35	1.25
36	.84	.78	36	1.45	1.31
37	.88	.82	37	1.56	1.38
38	.92	.86	38	1.68	1.45
39	.97	.90	39	1.81	1.52
40	1.03	.95	40	1.95	1.60
41	1.09	1.00	41	2.12	1.73
42	1.17	1.05	42	2.30	1.89
43	1.25	1.10	43	2.50	2.05
44	1.34	1.15	44	2.72	2.22
45	1.45	1.20	45	2.95	2.40
46	1.59	1.29	46	3.22	2.59
47	1.74	1.41	47	3.52	2.79
48	1.91	1.53	48	3.85	3.01
49	2.10	1.66	49	4.21	3.23
50	2.30	1.76	50	4.60	3.50
51	2.49	1.90	51	4.97	3.79
52	2.70	2.06	52	5.38	4.10
53	2.96	2.22	53	5.82	4.44
54	3.40	2.40	54	6.29	4.80
55	3.40	2.60	55	6.80	5.20
56	3.66	2.79	56	7.31	5.58
57	3.94	3.00	57	7.87	5.99
58	4.23	3.22	58	8.46	6.43
59	4.55	3.46	59	9.10	6.90
60	4.90	3.70	60	9.80	7.40
61	5.43	3.98	61	10.83	7.95
62	6.02	4.28	62	11.98	8.54
63	6.67	4.60	63	13.25	9.18
64	7.40	4.93	64	14.65	9.86
65	8.20	5.30	65	16.20	10.60

*Per $1,000 of coverage, per year
Source: Consumer Federation of America

FIGURE 14

Notes for figure 14:

- The table shows the premium rate per $1,000 of coverage. If you are buying a $100,000 policy, multiply the cost by 100 and add $60 (for the insurer's fixed policy expenses) to see the most that you should pay.

- Policies smaller than $100,000 cost a little more. Policies written for $500,000 and up cost a little less.

- Nonsmokers' rates are for preferred health risks.

- The relative rates for smokers keep rising as insurers see how fast the smokers are dying.

- Rates and companies may have changed by the time you read this. For an update, check the latest Consumer Federation of America guide *How to Save Money on Life Insurance* (available for a fee by calling 202-387-6121).

YEARLY PREMIUMS FOR
A $100,000 POLICY

Age	Term Insurance	Universal-Life Insurance	Whole-Life Insurance
30	$136	$ 590	$ 875
35	140	746	1,095
40	163	950	1,391
45	205	1,217	1,776
50	320	1,583	2,311
55	440	2,078	3,038
60	610	2,741	4,717
65	980	3,665	5,376

Source: Consumer Federation of America

FIGURE 15

HOME INSURANCE

If you own a home, condominium, or cooperative, you need enough of the right kind of insurance to cover it. If you rent, you need insurance to cover your possessions. Use this work sheet to sort out different types of policies available and determine the coverage you need.

HOME OWNER'S INSURANCE POLICY CHECKLIST

Feature	Recommendation	Policy 1 Coverage	Annual Premium Cost	Policy 2 Coverage	Annual Premium Cost
Type: HO-1, HO-2, HO-3, HO-4, HO-5, HO-6	See below, based on your type of home				
Value of Home	100% of replacement cost				
Property Insurance	Replacement cost				
Liability Insurance	$300,000+				
Deductibles	Highest you can afford				
Total Premium Cost		$		$	

FIGURE 16

How to fill out the work sheet

1. Type: Different types of policies exist for house owners, condominium or cooperative owners, and renters.

House Policies
House owners have four types of policies from which to choose: all provide limited coverage for personal belongings in your home:

HO-1 policies require that cause of loss be specifically named in your policy. For example, if your furnace explodes and destroys your home, "explosion" must be listed.

HO-2 policies typically cover explosion, fire, storms, theft, vandalism, and the like, but the cause of damage must be listed in the policy.

HO-3 policies are different in that they cover everything except what the policy specifically excludes—usually earthquakes, floods, termites, and rodents.

HO-5 policies offer the same coverage on the building as HO-3 but add more coverage on the contents. For most people, the benefits of HO-5 are not worth the cost, and they are better off with HO-3.

Condominium and Cooperative Policies
Condominium owners are covered by HO-6 policies; the coverage includes personal property. Condo owners must make sure their policies cover anything that the condominium association's master policy does not cover. Cooperative coverages do not apply because of the nature of cooperative ownership.

Renter Policies
Apartment renters are covered by HO-4 policies, which cover the contents of the apartment.

2. Value of home: You must base your insurance on the replacement cost of your home, not its market value. The market value of your home could be higher than the replacement cost of your home if your home has a lot of hand-crafted touches in it. Some insurance companies offer guaranteed replacement: if you insure your home for 100 percent of the value determined by the insurance company, your home will be replaced regardless of the rebuilding cost. If your policy has no such clause, you will receive only up to the amount of the policy.

3. Property insurance: Property insurance covers dwelling, other structures on your property, personal property including the contents of your home, landscaping, and additional living expenses you might incur if you have to move out of your home while it is being repaired after an accident. Usually you select the amount of coverage for your dwelling, and the amounts of the other coverages are a percentage of that. For example, if your dwelling is covered for $100,000, typically your personal property covered would be 50 percent of that, or $50,000. Check with your agent for details; if you need more for personal property or other categories, it can be added.

4. Liability insurance: This covers incidents such as somebody slipping and injuring himself on your property, or your dog biting somebody. Standard amount is $100,000, but for a small fee most companies will increase it to $300,000.

5. Deductibles: Getting the highest you can afford is best; $500 is typical, but check with your agent, and be aware that you must pay that amount before insurance coverage begins.

AUTO INSURANCE

Auto insurance is the type of insurance you are most likely to own. Most states require licensed drivers who own cars to be insured. Your exposure to liability is enormously high when you drive a car, and instead of just getting the minimum insurance required by the state, you should carefully determine the coverage you need. Use the work sheet and explanation for figure 17.

AUTO INSURANCE POLICY CHECKLIST

Feature	Recommendation	Policy 1 Coverage	Annual Premium Cost	Policy 2 Coverage	Annual Premium Cost
Bodily injury, liability, and property damage	100/300/50 (at least)				
Medical payments	$25,000				
Uninsured/ underinsured motorist	100/300/50				
Collision	Highest deductible you can handle				
Comprehensive	Highest deductible you can handle				
Towing and rental	Optional				
Total Premium Cost		$		$	

FIGURE 17

How to fill out the work sheet

1. Bodily injury and property liability damage: The injury portion covers anyone other than yourself for injuries caused by you. Covered expenses are medical payments, rehabilitation expenses, lost income, and compensation for pain and suffering. The property portion protects against damage to someone else's property, such as automobile, landscaping, or home. Most insurance experts recommend minimum levels of 25/50/10. Those numbers represent $25,000 injury to one person in an accident, maximum of $50,000 per accident for injuries, and $10,000 damage to property. You should, however, consider at least 100/300/50 if you can afford it, or if you have substantial assets to protect, consider 250/500 for bodily injury.

2. Medical payments: This covers medical expenses for you and your passengers for a defined period, usually a year. You might want it because your passengers may not have any other coverage of their own. Recommended limit of $25,000.

3. Uninsured/underinsured motorist: This covers you, your family, and your passengers if you are injured by a hit-and-run driver or if the other driver has no or inadequate insurance. Recommended limits of 100/300/50.

4. Collision: This covers damage to your car when you hit an object. It can be very expensive and is not usually worth the cost if your car is older. Coverage is only for the depreciated value of your car. If coverage costs 10 percent or more of the car's value, or if your car is more than five years old, you probably should not have it, but some lenders may require it.

5. Comprehensive: Pays for most other types of damage such as theft, vandalism, or storm damage. Coverage recommendation is the same as for collision.

6. Towing or rental: This pays the cost of towing your car from the site of an accident or for renting a car if yours is stolen or in an accident. Coverage is cheap, but you might have it from an auto club or in your collision or comprehensive coverage.

NOTES

Chapter 11

1. Mike Orkin, *Can You Win? The Real Odds for Casino Gambling, Sports Betting and Lotteries* (New York: W. H. Freeman & Co., 1991).
2. James Walsh, *True Odds* (Santa Monica: Merritt, 1996).
3. Ibid.
4. "Facts About Las Vegas" (1996 statistics from the Las Vegas Convention and Visitors Authority).
5. Ken Winters, Randy Stinchfield, and Jayne Fulkerson, *Adolescent Survey of Gambling Behavior in Minnesota: A Benchmark* (Center for Addiction Studies, University of Minnesota-Duluth and Center for Adolescent Substance Abuse, University of Minnesota: 1990).
6. Mary Herring and Timothy Bledsoe, "A Model of Lottery Participation: Demographics, Context and Attitudes," *Policy Studies Journal,* 22 (Summer 1994), 245–57.
7. Daniel J. Brown, Dennis O. Kaldenberg, and Beverly A. Browne, "Socio-economic Status and Playing the Lotteries," *Sociology and Social Research,* 76, no. 3 (April 1992), 161–67.
8. Frank Fahrenkopf, interviewed by Phil Donahue on *Donahue,* 21 November 1995.
9. Mary O. Borg, Paul M. Mason, and Stephen L. Shapiro, "The Incidence of Taxes on Casino Gambling: Exploiting the Tired and Poor," *American Journal of Economics and Sociology,* 50, no. 3 (July 1991), 323–32.
10. John Warren Kindt, "The Business-Economic Impacts of Licensed Casino Gambling in West Virginia: Short-Term Gain but Long-Term Pain." This report was included in the publication *The National Impact of Casino Gambling Proliferation: Hearing Before the House Committee on Small Business* (103rd Congress, 2d session 77 [1994]).

TOPIC INDEX

(Figure numbers shown can be found in back of book)

— 223 —

SCRIPTURE INDEX

More Financial Insight By Charles Ross

Your Commonsense Guide to Personal Financial Planning

Financial expert Charles Ross provides sound, practical advice on how to budget, protect, save, and invest money. This down-to-earth resource is for anyone, young or old, who needs information on financial basics.

0-7852-7222-4 • Mass Market Paperback • 228 pages